Dark Prophets of Hope

DOSTOEVSKY • SARTRE • CAMUS • FAULKNER

Jean Kellogg

LOYOLA   UNIVERSITY   PRESS

Chicago, 1975

LOYOLA UNIVERSITY PRESS

Printed in the United States of America

LIBRARY OF CONGRESS
CATALOGING IN PUBLICATION DATA

Kellogg, Jean Defrees, 1916-
  Dark prophets of hope—Dostoevsky, Sartre, Camus, Faulkner.

  Includes bibliographical references.
    1. Camus, Albert, 1913-1960.   2. Dostoevskiĭ, Fedor Mikhaĭl-
ovich, 1821-1881.   3. Faulkner, William, 1897-1962.   4. Sartre,
Jean-Paul, 1905-   5. Literature—Philosophy.   I. Title.

PN771.K38   809′.933′1   75-5697

ISBN 0-8294-0234-9 (cloth) ; ISBN 0-8294-0243-8 (paper)

CONTENTS

vi Dark Prophets of Hope

TO

NATHAN SCOTT

"Art is not only man's most supreme expression;
it is also the salvation of mankind."

WILLIAM FAULKNER

It seems to many that to live in our time is to inhabit a kaleidoscope in which bits of fragmented religion, shards of old ideals, scraps of once-upon-a-time brotherhood— your Catholicism, for example, or your Lutheranism, or your ethnic identity, or even your profession, whose part in contributing to society you shared or thought you shared with similarly oriented people—everything is in dissolution. Those Catholics who today look back with wonder on the papal power of the nineteenth century would find the same emotion in modern Hindus in regard to Brahminism or modern Russians in regard to their Party leaders. How to comprehend the chaos that seems to be upon us?

The gifted African writer, Chinua Achebe, in his compassionate novel, *Things Fall Apart*, created a moving portrait of an Ibo tribe in its state of dissolution a century ago. The novel owed much of its impact to its parallel with the situation in which the Western world finds itself at

1

present. There are symbolic similarities which are startling. There are also startling differences.

The wisdom of the Ibo resided in nine masked elders, who in story were ancestors of the tribe. The "story" was in fact quite accurate. The past was truly alive in the maskers who maintained the traditions by which the tribe lived. The future lived in them also, for they guided the consensus of all tribal decisions. In the maskers the tribe not only renewed its being "in illo tempore" so that their gods lived and moved the people, but justice was dispensed, the crops were sown, and the harvest arrived. As long as this storied coherence held together past and future, as long as this self-understanding continued and developed, the tribe advanced, the people endured, and their center held. Chaos was loosed upon their world only when the people were unable to become aware of the signs of fragmentation within their tribal culture, a dissolution in process long before the white man arrived. In the end the people found themselves incapable of maintaining their own culture in simultaneity with that of the new time.

For us, however, the sense of chaos is keen. Not only that, but there are signs which indicate that there may be evolving in us something very like simultaneity between an order of the past and an order of the future. Our center is not dissolving, and "story" may be precisely where we can see not only how the center has been held but also how it is forming itself anew. We in the West have taken story with particular seriousness in the last hundred years. In each generation millions have been moved by certain books regarded as no less than prophetic, in the sense that they have been received as carrying truth beyond ordinary vision. The long list of prophetic writers in the West runs from major prophets like Dostoevsky and Sartre to lesser figures like Hesse and Castenada. It is folly to take lightly the phenomenon of the reverent attention given to such writers in recent decades. When so many people are finding meaning, there must be some reason for them to do so.

For a long time there has been a virtual epidemic of prophetic writers. There has been in the arts no flowering of similar magnitude since that last great era of change, the transition from the Middle Ages to the Renaissance. Yet in the nineteenth and twentieth centuries, writers regarded as uncannily accurate in their sense of the shape of things to come have been a center of attention for millions, and still have never generated any specialized critical approach able to distinguish them from other authors. One object of this essay is to make a modest start in developing tools of analysis suitable to this kind of art.

To be considered a prophetic writer in the context of this essay, an author must have a coherent and compelling view of the human condition and must have obtained a large and influential following. The most important object is not literary analysis. The purpose is to examine four central and significant visions of our time and indicate an important trend they have in common, a trend toward what is called in this essay "simultaneity of opposites." Most people today, conscious that they are living in an era of the dissolution of nearly all familiar forms, want to know how and why the dissolution has come about, and what new forms, if any, are to come into being, or if our future is to be—as many appear to believe—simply a struggle of all against all until a rigid world dictatorship shall rise and force the entire race into some type of compulsory ant heap, without space for private integrity or opportunity for individual genius. Those are precisely the matters that have occupied the prophetic writers of the last hundred years and given them their appeal. And, when we look at the amazing similarity between their visions, when we consider the correspondence with what has actually come to pass, and when we regard their view of humanity's future and the functioning of what is here called simultaneity, the reaction we shall feel is not confusion or loss of hope but something very like that combination of understanding and steadfastness which Camus showed in *The Plague* as the goal of his hero, Tarrou. It is a frame of mind able, I believe, to overcome even what Abraham Maslow has called the "subculture of despair," so ingrained in our society in this time of fragmentation between contradictions. A new state of consciousness that can tolerate contradictions, and even draw vitality from them, is forming. And in that state of consciousness man will not only endure, he will prevail.

CHAPTER I

Alienation and Solidarity
Interlocking Opposites

In the ninth and tenth centuries Vikings from the Baltic began to sail down the water roads to Byzantium. Along the Don and the Dnieper they planted settlements on the plains and in the forests, as they felled the giant birches for reprovisioning centers and outposts for their ever richer fur trade.

These Vikings, called simply Rus, were the founders of Russia. They stamped its character from the beginning into a division between rulers and ruled: the indigenous population bound to its forests and plains, and the privileged Rus mobile in their ships. It was a breach that would never be healed. Like most of the tragic divisions in modern Russia, it started in the beginning.

In 989 came the conversion of Prince Vladimir of Kiev to Byzantine Christianity. When Byzantium split with Rome in the eleventh and twelfth centuries,[1] Russian contempt for the way of the popes and Russian commitment to

5

the way of the patriarchs also became part of the Russian character. Rome, in the view of her Russian critics, was a kingdom among the kingdoms of this world. The Pope was an earthly prince, entering into treaties, maintaining armies and alliances. Byzantium, on the other hand, was a kingdom of unearthly glory whose spiritual lord was not an earthly prince but Christ himself. Rome, as the Russian and Byzantine mind saw her, had betrayed the Christian spiritual ideal to the forces of the earth. Indeed the Italian "Rome" was no longer Rome at all, the city of Christ which had consecrated the heirs of Peter. Byzantium was "Rome," the second Rome, taking up the torch where the first had let it fall.

The difference in outlook may be seen in Italian and Byzantine painting. While still deep in the Middle Ages, Italian painters of sacred subjects began to open them toward the world. Behind the compassionate Madonna and her Child, perhaps between two pillars or out a window, would be seen a vista leading into a tiny landscape of trees and flowers. Painted in exquisite detail, it symbolized the separated presence of earthy everyday life. At first it was carefully miniaturized but later grew in importance until by the Renaissance the Madonna seemed a woman like any other except for her greater beauty. Quite different was the Russian Virgin with her Child. Behind them would remain, as behind all Russian sacred painting as long as Russian sacred painting existed, the solid golden background characteristic of Byzantine art. The Madonna and her Child stood directly in God's golden light that through them divinized all humanity.

In 1453 Constantinople fell to the Turks. Sophia Paleologus, niece of the last Byzantine emperor, crossed Russia to marry Ivan III, Duke of Moscow. It was a magnificent moment, that progress of Sophia across Russia. Her little group of merely human escorts moved across that vast landscape like incarnate tradition moving forever, and yet forever abiding, like figures in one of the golden Byzantine mosaics. Moscow now became the third Rome, noblest and last upholder of the sacred mission that the second Rome had served. The rulers of the solidifying Russian kingdom soon took the Roman imperial seal of the two-headed eagle and the title of Tsar. The Russian Caesar, consecrated as the new heir to Constantine, now lived on the water roads.

The sense of a holy mission was increased by the fact that since the thirteenth century the Russians had been civilization's outpost against the Mongols. The Russian mounted knight is a significant figure, so heavily armed that in him the Russians may be said to have invented the first tank. Ten, twenty of the lightly clad barbarians might fall before his single sword. To put into the field such a cataphract was enormously costly. The Russian people were taxed, fled their obligations, and finally fled the land. They were caught, punished for their treason to the holy mission of Holy Russia, and the long shadow formed which would end with a whole population bound to its soil on pain of being regarded as guilty of dereliction from a sacred duty which was owed to all of mankind—a binding which has existed throughout Russian history. For a Russian to leave Russia is still a sin against the people.

By the time of the Russian Middle Ages, mobility increasingly distinguished the ruling from the ruled. By 1592, when the Mongol Horde had been replaced by other enemies, the peasants were transformed into serfs forbidden to leave their fields. Despite this fact or perhaps because of it, the Russian people were more than ever regarded as holy. They suffered for the Russian mission as heirs of Christ, and their suffering was analogous to the suffering of the crucified. Nowhere else in the world did suffering become so much an accepted, even a reverenced part of the fabric of life. Long before Dostoevsky analyzed this aspect of the Russian character, Russia was a nation of sadists and masochists, with most of the population tempted to one or the other, or both at the same time.

As the split between the ruling and the ruled spread ever wider, a compensation developed. The ruling class saw itself not as a class of privilege but as consecrated "men of service." Their service was given to Russia's sacred mission and Russia's suffering people. Under Peter the Great in the eighteenth century, the men of service accomplished superhuman feats of devotion. The first Count Tolstoy, in 1697, volunteered to go to Venice to learn Venetian shipbuilding. He returned with a treasury of knowledge. By heroic efforts to absorb European culture and technology, the Russia of Peter's time tried to overcome the backwardness of a nation torn by centuries of war with the barbarians, while Europe, sheltered from the barbarians by Russia, had forged ahead.

Under Peter and his successor Catherine, the men of service became organized into a gigantic administrative network. So vast a country required vast organization. The most enormous bureaucracy in the West shambled into birth. It was to survive alike the abolition of serfdom in 1861 and the Leninist revolution of 1917. Leaving behind the consecrated sense of mission and the efficiency of its beginnings, it would become, as far as anyone could see, the most unalterable and most inhuman aspect of the Russian condition.

Russia thus became the earliest of the modern massively bureaucratized states in the West, a fact which explains why so many of our modern spiritual diseases were first diagnosed there. A bureaucracy is a peculiar organism. In appearance tightly welded together, it is actually composed of discrete and viciously separated particles.

Nearly all the great Russian writers were such particles, alienated from functional participation or satisfying contribution to meaningful life. Pushkin was a landowner, a descendant of a Negro slave who had risen to be a general in the service of Peter the Great. Pushkin, idle and isolated, belonged to a class which in the proliferation of the bureaucracy had by his time lost all sense of mission or the possibility of effectiveness under the existing system. In a tragic demonstration of the violence which Dostoevsky was to examine as accompanying the loss of coherent community and meaningful life, Pushkin killed his best friend in a senseless duel and died himself in 1837 in a duel equally senseless. Meanwhile his liberal political opinions made him suspect to most of his class, though he was a hero to those who shared his perspectives and desired reform.

Dostoevsky was, like Pushkin, bred from the Russian bureaucracy. He was a son of an army doctor who was attached to a Moscow hospital as a civil servant. As such he was a member of the insignificant lower orders of Tsarist administration. Dostoevsky's father grew violent in his later years and indulged in such enormities of drunkenness and rape on his estate that he was murdered by his serfs, who in a mode particularly Russian first strangled him with vodka, crushed his genitals between their hands to punish him for his drunkenness and fornication, and then sent for a priest to administer the last rites. Dostoevsky himself early left the army engineering corps for which he had been trained. His aim was to write, to reflect somehow the rigid, atomized society in which he lived, perhaps to change it by his pen (his model was Balzac), and also possibly to change it by revolution. His life reflected the anguished confusion of his era. He was a compulsive gambler, an ex-Siberian exile turned Tsarist conservative, and a collector of news clippings about the social and psychological horror of moral disintegration that most fascinated him: child abuse. Dostoevsky was, not only in his youth but even in his later days of acceptance by the Tsar's advisers and popularity with Russian conservatives, always inwardly a "raskol," as cut off from the life and outlook of his hereditary class as was his character Raskolnikov, the "cut-off-one" in *Crime and Punishment*.

Dostoevsky's great contemporary, Tolstoy, was equally cut off. Unlike Dostoevsky he never became reconciled to autocracy but said—in a characteristically Russian inversion of the idea of life as sacred calling—that to pay taxes to the Tsar was treason to mankind. Yet with typically Russian ambivalence he was a landowner who expounded theories of organization both in his experiments on his estate at Yasnaya Polyana and in his books. In *Anna Karenina*, Levin, troubled by the condition of the serfs, separated himself and his family from the existence of aimless sociability ordinarily led by his class. On his own property Levin determined to create a model of true community. He would do away with hierarchic rule, tyranny, and flogging. A happy and harmonious peasantry would labor spontaneously together. He himself went out into the fields. Success in his project, however, eluded Levin, as it eluded Tolstoy. All his life Tolstoy dreamed of fleeing his estates to establish a truly human life in peasant hut or "isba," to share the labor of the suffering masses. Meanwhile he was forced to live on his estates by the family exigency of being father to eleven children and by the social exigency of being Russia's greatest writer, a world famous prophet of Utopia to come, which would be brought about by a social transformation in which all would come to share the wisdom of the uncorrupted peasantry. All people would work with their own hands; no man would live on another's labor. According to Tolstoy's philosophy, the current of history was carried by the good and the simple, the people of the earth like the general Kutuzov and the peasant Platon Karataev in *War and Peace*. The transformation he looked forward to was determined by historical forces.

Tolstoy lived according to his beliefs as best he was able—an effort that resulted in ironic contradictions. During the day he labored with his hands cobbling shoes. In the evenings he climbed the stairs from his basement room to preside over his wife's table (in later life he had placed the greater part of his properties in her name), and with his butler behind his chair he received international visitors and fulfilled his role as heir to the first Count Tolstoy, whose own service of humanity had been without his descendant's troubled perspectives. Finally, at eighty-two, in the last days of his life, Tolstoy sought his long-anticipated isba and solidarity with the Russian people. He set off secretly on a train with his favorite daughter and his physician, only to be taken ill and die slowly in a railroad way station, while public bulletins on his health were issued to a breathless world.

The whole odyssey is a prototype of a modern madness. A false life desperately seeks authenticity. Isolation struggles toward functioning community—unreachable in the circumstances of the time. In Tolstoy's novels, as alienation rises, so does the longing for solidarity. Pierre Bezuhov is one example. Levin is another. Each endures lifelong torment. One must pity and admire the dying Tolstoy in the railroad station, but one cannot fail to see the tragic irony. Tolstoy remains Tolstoy, forever unassimilable in the sacred masses of unknown Platon Karataevs.

Although Tolstoy never met Dostoevsky, he disliked Dostoevsky's work, with the significant exception of *The House of the Dead*, Dostoevsky's account of his Siberian exile. But it was in Siberia that Dostoevsky lost his revolutionary idealism. He had been sentenced for implication in a plot to disseminate liberal propaganda, and he spent four years in conditions unimaginable in their horror:

All the floor boards are rotten; on the ground filth lies half an inch thick; every instant you are in danger of slipping and falling. The small windows are so frozen over that there is no time in the day when it is possible to read. There is another half inch of ice on the panes. The ceilings drip, there are draughts everywhere. We are packed like herrings in a barrel. The stove is heated with six logs of wood, no heat, the ice scarcely melts in the room—and so it goes on all through the winter.

In the same room the prisoners wash their clothes, and everything is drenched. No way to move. From dawn to dusk we are forbidden to leave the hut to satisfy our needs, for the doors are bolted. A large wooden trough is placed at the entrance, and the stench is intolerable. All the prisoners stink like pigs; they say it is impossible not to behave like pigs. since "we are living beings."[2]

After his release from prison Dostoevsky spent five more years as a Siberian exile. His abandonment of belief in revolution came not from any chastening effect of his punishment but from observations in his surroundings. He saw human nature at its most elemental, evil inextricably mingled with good. His belief came to be that no revolution could do more than change one group at the top for another. What was needed was evolution of the soul and heart. Solzhenitsyn, who was for many years a political prisoner of the new Russian autocracy, came to much the same conclusion.[3] Tolstoy disowned autocracy. Dostoevsky's feelings were different. They were opposite types. Tolstoy was basically a determinist and a socialist. Dostoevsky was a believer in human free will as God-given. Yet paradoxically Dostoevsky was a follower of Tsarism. It was because of his paradoxes, his psychological obscurity that Tolstoy objected to Dostoevsky's fiction, while to the latter Tolstoy may have seemed superficial. In *The Brothers Karamazov* Dostoevsky sneered at Tolstoy's famous realism, calling it cuff button accuracy.[4]

This sort of accuracy Dostoevsky probably thought unimportant. Certainly he did not practice it. Alyosha in *The Brothers Karamazov* was nineteen on one page, twenty on another, and the birth date of Dmitri was obscure if not impossible.[5] But Dostoevsky understood, as Tolstoy never did, the inherent contradiction of the human condition in Russia. His life in Siberia and his natural acuteness in matters of psychology gave him special entry into complex darknesses of the human heart as they were increased by what he called the ant heap, which would not be relieved by the simple absence of the Tsar. Tolstoy realized that the solitary and walled-off human particle, whose existence was confined to the class divisions and the meshes of the solidly bureaucratized state, had the agonizing anonymity and personal powerlessness that has since spread to the rest of the world. Tolstoy, however, also had his belief that this mutual feeding of opposite forces, isolation and bureaucracy, anonymous helplessness and state giganticism, was curable by removal of the bureaucracy. Historical determinism would exalt the instinctively wise, the Russian people of the earth. These portions of Tolstoy's beliefs explain why, in 1970, my Intourist guide, who could not even point out the Moscow birthplace of Dostoevsky, took me to Tolstoy's distant Yasnaya Polyana, "Sunlit Meadows," as to a national shrine. Before the gates, busloads of ten- and twelve-year-old Komsomols in identical white shirts and red kerchiefs were being discharged to be marched reverently through the premises. No one would have been more horrified than Tolstoy at the sight of that swarm of identically clad children sent out to be indoctrinated by the new Russian bureaucracy into acquiescence to the complex pretenses necessary for modern Russian ant heap living and ant heap psychology, all embodied in new myths, of which he himself was one.

CHAPTER II

Suffering and Psychic Blackmail
Dostoevsky
and Sadomasochism

"Ant heap" was Dostoevsky's term, not Tolstoy's. For Dostoevsky the ant heap was primarily the shape of the future,[1] but he saw many of its characteristics in the Russia of his time. The ant heap frame of mind was one of the most conspicuous elements of his vision of the Russian condition in his masterpiece of 1879, *The Brothers Karamazov*. In the ant heap of nineteenth-century Russia, which was the background of Dostoevsky's epic, people felt themselves devoid of that individual recognition which in Dostoevsky's view the human personality had to have in order to construct meaningful existence.

Dostoevsky drew such a person in the eldest Karamazov brother, Dmitri, a young army officer who had been defrauded of his inheritance by his father, and who was so

completely non-oriented to his army career that drunkenness and rebellion had on at least one occasion caused him
to be reduced to the ranks. In the garrison town where
Dmitri, promoted once more, was stationed, a proud young
woman from Moscow, the daughter of Dmitri's command-
ing officer, came to take up residence. Katya was regarded
by the town as its most desirable young woman. There was
a strong resemblance between Dmitri and Katya. Each
lived within a shell of glamorous personality enclosing an
inner self bitterly insecure and feeling in danger of obliteration. Dmitri was suffering from a sense of wrong and
defeat, as a man cheated of his inheritance by circumstances he could neither comprehend nor redress. Katya,
like many spirited women in a world dominated by masculine institutions, compulsively made herself challenging
to every male and entered into battle for psychic ascendancy. She chose a wonderfully effective way to challenge
Dmitri. Deliberately she, the area's most eligible female,
took no notice of him, the most sought-after male. Dmitri
Karamazov was not the man to overlook *that!*

Soon Dmitri heard that Katya's father, the Colonel,
might be short in his regimental accounts. Dmitri dropped
a word to Katya's meek and unattractive elder half sister
that all could be rectified if "you would like to send me
your young lady secretly."[2] What ensued almost immediately was the sadomasochistic phenomenon Dostoevsky
called "laceration." Both Katya and Dmitri had what Dostoevsky saw as the goal of all persons who felt themselves
denied the meaningful recognition they desired. In any
personal relationship, each sought recognition from and

dominance over the other. The struggle was complex, ruthless, and full of psychic violence.

The shortage in the Colonel's accounts was in danger of being discovered. Katya arrived at Dmitri's door, pale, out of breath, and ready to offer herself to him. She was the classic exemplar of the noble self-sacrificing daughter who gives up her honor to save her father. But in this struggle for recognition and dominance, Dmitri was at this time more skillful than Katya. Only for a moment did he think he would recognize her in her chosen role of heroine, let her—in Dostoevsky's term—achieve the deliciously self-"lacerating" identity of self-sacrificer as he possessed himself of her physically. In that way she would have established her ascendancy over him forever. What he did was reverse the roles and seize heroism for himself by leaving the lovely Katya still a virgin. He handed her with a low bow the last of his inheritance, a five thousand ruble note. With a deep obeisance the overwhelmed Katya left. Physically she was untouched. Psychically she was crushed by the superiority seized from her just at the moment when she had thought herself most armored in superiority. As for Dmitri, he was in such a state of ecstasy that he almost stabbed himself in the joy of the moment.

Time passed and Katya inherited money. She became engaged to Dmitri. No matter how unfaithful he was to her with the "fallen woman," Grushenka, Katya resolved that she would nobly bear his "vileness." Her goal became quite clear when she said that in her suffering faithfulness she would be for Dmitri "a god to whom he can pray."[3] Of course she did not "love" Dmitri at all. What she loved, as

Dmitri pointed out, was "her own virtue,"[4] her own ascendancy. Later in their lives Dmitri was to speak of her as a "woman of great wrath."[5] She was indeed.

Katya deliberately put temptation in Dmitri's way. He stole money from her which he spent on Grushenka. Dmitri then despised himself in an agony of bitterness. By succumbing to Katya's cleverly managed temptation, he had lost his greatest treasure, his honor as a Russian officer, the one identity his disinherited condition afforded him. Despising himself, he was utterly isolated, for a man whose pattern of relationship must be dominance could not enter into a relationship with anyone—Grushenka or anyone else however beloved—as long as he believed himself to be "vile." Katya, who had passed on him this sentence of "vileness," was equally isolated, for she was pretending to love Dmitri when actually she hated him and pretending to serve him when actually she was crucifying him.

Thus "laceration" acted as a force of isolation in the complex Russian world, where people who sought the solidarity with others that recognition would have given them found recognition and solidarity forever eluding them. To achieve recognition, the Russian victim of alienation characteristically sacrificed himself or herself, ostensibly for the good of others. Such sacrifices were not "sacrifices" at all but "laceration." Suffering became, as with Katya, psychic violence against the chosen antagonist. Better to suffer than to give up the sense of wrong that assured you of your identity and of your dominance over the one who had wronged you, and whose identity, as his greatest treasure, you sought to destroy in order to achieve your own.

In the town of Skotoprigonyevsk[6] (the literal transla-
tion was "beast-pen"), where Dostoevsky set his story,
there was a certain Captain Snegiryov, an agent of Dmitri's
father in collecting Dmitri's debts. Dmitri had mercilessly
humiliated Captain Snegiryov by dragging him out of a
tavern and beating him. Snegiryov was unable to challenge
Dmitri to a duel because he was the sole support of an in-
valid wife and daughter. Snegiryov's little son Ilusha attempted to avenge the family by "laceration." Because
Dostoevsky saw disturbed children as more easily understood prototypes of disturbed adults and studied them with
the earnestness born of unbearable compassion, it was typical that in his novel he should reflect laceration in a child.
Ilusha was a ten-year-old whose schoolmates had asserted
their dominance by alternately ignoring and bullying him.
Their taunts were directed at Ilusha's father's supposed
cowardice before Dmitri. Ilusha in response threw stones
at Dmitri's brother, Alyosha. The child tried desperately
to get Alyosha to give him recognition by striking him, but
when Alyosha, who was a monk, bore Ilusha's attacks without retaliation, the boy gave a cry of despair and ran off.
He had been defeated in his hope of identity as a sufferer
who bravely endured the injustice of his suffering, and so
prevailed in a psychic duel and rose to the challenge his
father had not been able to meet.

Later Katya, seeking as ever to sacrifice herself for
Dmitri, sent money to the destitute Snegiryov to make up
for the wrong done to the Captain by Dmitri. The bearer
of the money was Alyosha. Snegiryov's little son, Ilusha,
was now ill with fever, so when Alyosha gave Snegiryov

the money the impoverished ex-officer was beside himself
with joy. He would buy medicines for Ilusha. He would establish himself in another town where his past would be
unknown. His alienation, and that of his family, could give
way to meaningful relationships for them all. But Dostoevsky was an accurate measurer of the values he uncovered
in what he called the "ant heap." As soon as Snegiryov
came to himself and really weighed the security of a promised job and the prospect of health for the people he gen-
uinely loved as possibilities against the certainties of his
present identity of a man with an unrighted wrong—who
related to others as a sufferer crushed by undeserved suffering at the hands of an oppressor whose "vileness"
Snegiryov indicted by his very existence—he arrived at
what was for a person in that time, place, and circumstance
the only viable solution. He threw the notes into the snow
and trampled on them. He had almost been tricked by
Alyosha's goodwill, but he had recovered himself in time.
Only the most complete assurance of real power can make
a victim give up the perverse power of his identity as victim. Only the fullest prospect of a pride that is to be not
only respected but exalted will make a victim abandon his
grip on the distorted pride of the insulted and injured.
When Captain Snegiryov finally consents on a later day to
be given the bank notes, what persuades him is the argu-
ment that he is doing Katya and Alyosha and those who
have injured him a favor by accepting the money.

Snegiryov or anyone like him is always reluctant to
give up the advantages of laceration. In the pattern of laceration the sufferer inflicts suffering on those who have

caused him to suffer and so establishes both identity and superiority. There can be no sweeter revenge for one obliterated in an ant heap—either as Snegiryov was by poverty and insult, or as Katya was, first by the subjection of her position as a woman with pride and a drive for dominance that could find no satisfaction in her society,[7] and then by the humiliation inflicted by Dmitri. By conferring on her the "benefit" of his five thousand rubles, Dmitri degraded her in a way which she could never forget and which she spent the rest of her life trying to avenge.

In evaluating such a diagnosis of the human condition as is contained within Dostoevsky's dramatization of laceration, one must do more than simply admire the writer's excellence as a psychologist dealing with the individuals of his time and place. Dostoevsky clearly belongs to the type of writer called in our introduction prophetic. He has held enormous audiences throughout the world and wielded immense influence. Why? Were his insights not only keen, have they also been found accurate? If so, was the accuracy confined to his epoch and his nation or was it in some sense universal? More important, has it been seen to grow and define itself as time has gone on?

Anyone who carefully considers the modern scene must realize that since Dostoevsky wrote of laceration in Russia of the mid-nineteenth century the condition has become endemic. Today racial minorities, ghetto dwellers, displaced persons, people in underdeveloped nations, prisoners, habitual criminals, plus untold thousands of "ordinary" persons somehow "on the bottom" or made to suffer unjustly, experience the perverse compensations of laceration. Part of the syndrome is what Ilusha knew so well. The "good" Karamazov brother, Alyosha, could be held just as guilty of the wrongs done to the lacerated as the "bad" Karamazov brother, Dmitri, who actually performed the action. Alyosha knew this too, and willingly carried the bank notes that were to get Captain Snegiryov and his wrongs off the backs of the Karamazovs, who for the lacerated were a single entity. The entire rest of the world is always a single entity to the lacerated. The good may always be blackmailed for the bad, as Ilusha attempted to blackmail the innocent Alyosha. In the conscience of the lacerated, it is justifiable to take hostages anywhere. In fact, the more innocent the hostage is in the eyes of the rest of the world, the more effectively the lacerated proclaims his identity as a sufferer. That he may justly inflict suffering on anyone anywhere simply proves who he is, this inflicter of indiscriminate suffering. He is the most wronged person in the world. Before his sufferings, the purest innocence pales. The happenstance bystanders shot down by terrorists at random in an airport, the young diplomat killed as hostage for his country's "ruling class"—such victims, by their innocence, measure how wronged the lacerated are, since their wrongs are clearly what compels them to these actions. Everyone on earth is less wronged than the lacerated. Everyone is on the same footing, and there are no innocent except those on the bottom who are the lacerated themselves. In the pattern shown by Dostoevsky in Katya, Ilusha, and Captain Snegiryov, the lacerated would not for anything give up their laceration. It is their one complete identity and their one source of dominance in a world which crushes them. Since laceration is everywhere in any massed ant heap, and since the phenomenon is one that is obviously very much with us, it may be interesting to try to distinguish between various species within the modern type and apply Dostoevsky's prophecies further.

Some criminals seem to use laceration, as do some drug addicts. If an attempt is made to help them take their place in conformist society, many prefer to nourish a sense of wrong and use it to regard the non-criminal or non-drug-using world with scorn. Frequently they believe, perhaps with accuracy, that the conformist world once did or is doing them an injustice. Continuing to commit crimes, use drugs, or whatever their deviation may be, they practice a self-lacerating revenge on that world and by demonstrating their scorn of its norms they establish a sense of inner superiority that can be very sweet. To accept anything that the conformist world could offer in the way of jobs or "respectability" would be regarded as surrender, and also would not be nearly as satisfying as a means of identity and superiority. The early portions of the autobiography of Malcolm X reveal this state of consciousness. Malcolm X was a man who fought his way out of the psychological traps of America in the nineteen-forties, but to do so took all his remarkable insight and strength of character. Malcolm X is rightly regarded as a hero by large segments of the ant heap population in the contemporary United States.

A more difficult mode of laceration to escape from seems to be that of the man or woman who protests not merely his or her own suffering but that of a group or mass. Negotiation may be all but impossible between these representatives of the mass and the conformist rulers of society. Nothing that could be offered would detach them from the cause for which they are willing, indeed eager, to suffer, because by their suffering they fling in the teeth of the world an accusation of injustice and wrong. Their cause is often one which any sensible and unbiased observer must acknowledge as just, or at least so they believe. For this reason they seek maximum publicity. Nehru and Gandhi in prison or on a hunger strike are examples of how effectively this type of laceration could be used.

The species of lacerated person to which Nehru and Gandhi belonged, however, became much more difficult to deal with forty years later. Liberation of India from colonial rule was hard to bring about but not impossible, particularly since India was beginning to show signs of becoming an expense rather than a source of profit. In the nineteen-seventies, however, the conditions in South American slums, the plight of the Palestinian refugees, and other similar injustices are so interlocked within the politico-economic framework of the shrinking world that they are enormously difficult to change. The passive resistance of a Nehru or a Gandhi has given way to the active terrorism of the Tupamaros, the Irish IRA, Palestinian activists who cling to terror as a weapon, and others ready to attack injustice by willingly accepting suffering and willingly giving their lives. The abundant and growing terrorism of what are virtually suicide squads attests the growth of this use of laceration as a means of psychological attack. Such people are capable of feats of astonishing fanaticism or of great heroism—how you see them depends on your point of view. The Buddhist monks who publicly burned themselves to death to protest the Vietnam War were examples.

Mass laceration also exists, and is even more complicated to deal with than the laceration of an individual who represents a mass. It may help to clarify this sort of situation by drawing a simple analogy from familiar private situations. Almost everyone knows a family group containing one member who has been wronged, and who not only refuses to let the wrong be righted but so engineers circumstances that wrongs continue. By this means he or she proclaims identity and moral superiority as an unjustly suffering victim of a despicable group whose (again to borrow a word from Dostoevsky) "vileness" the victim establishes by the conditions of his or her very existence. Exactly that situation prevailed for more than a quarter of a century in the Palestinian refugee camps. In Europe after the Second World War, the refugee camps for displaced persons were emptied as quickly as possible and their populations absorbed by the free nations of the West. But the Arab nations refused to take steps to resettle Palestinian refugees. The West after World War II had no reason to keep the displaced persons' camps in existence. Hitler was defeated; there was no point in maintaining concentrations of misery that most saw as accusing a wrong gone by into the past.[8] But the Arab nations had every reason, and so had the Palestinians themselves, to keep from dissolution the camps with their atrocious conditions. The Palestinians demonstrated to themselves daily by their suffering the wrong done to them by Israel. To Arab extremists, the camps proclaimed the only terms on which it was possible to proceed, the only terms on which the sufferings of the Palestinians would cease: the obliteration of Israel as a nation. The innocence of the Palestinians was used to strengthen the attack. Children were being born in these camps. Whole generations had known no other way of life —simply because of the natural refusal to be dispersed as a nation. The inflicter of suffering as undeserved as this must indeed be regarded as "vile." Anything done to any Israeli, or anything done to anyone in a world which condoned these conditions, was justifiable. The lacerated are always single-minded about innocence. They see it only in themselves.

What is the aim of laceration? Why prolong and re-prolong self-lacerating injustices? The aim is as single as laceration's view of its own innocence. Laceration prepares psychically for fury. Captain Snegiryov could release his laceration only by destroying the whole of his little world as rage burst upon him and he flung the bank notes into the snow. Modern lacerations operate on a larger scale. The destruction of all humanity or the unhinging of the universe itself would scarcely be sufficient release for some of the lacerations building in the late twentieth century.

There are areas in which laceration has not yet developed into a psychic explosive. These areas include many parts of what was once known as the third world, those nations not allied with any of the great powers. The suffering in these areas is frightful. It is also widely known, because of television and because of the travel which business, educational, and cultural exchange make part of modern life.

In 1970 I was in India. We arrived in Calcutta at dawn, just as the carts were going through the streets to pick up those among the people sleeping on the sidewalks who had died in the night. The wagons, incredibly old, rickety, wooden-wheeled incarnations of an agonized past, were drawn not by bullocks but by old men, whose wrinkled, stoical, time-etched emaciated faces beneath their tattered turbans made them seem as ancient as the carts they drew. Their clothes were rags, the uniform of the poor in India, where most of the population lives at or below the subsistence level. They were barefoot except for a few lucky ones who had scraps of old rubber tires tied to the soles of their feet with fraying twine. They leaned into the shafts with a weariness that spoke of the anguish of centuries.

Every few yards a cart would stop. Behind them were walking in pairs the more vigorous of these tragic avatars of death. One of them would step to the sidewalk and touch on the shoulder one of the rag-clad sleeping throng who was not awake and stirring in the pale light of the new day. If the one touched did not move, the men would stoop briefly, feel the wrists, raise the eyelids, and then taking feet and shoulders would sling the corpse on top of those already in the wagon as the grim procession moved on. Several of those I saw in the death carts were children.

Only birth control or miracle can mitigate India's agony. The Congress Government was making great efforts to propagandize for a lower birthrate. On the walls of every city and every village we saw the omnipresent sign: "Small family, happy family," and for the illiterate a drawing of two adults with two children. But birth control will never prevail in India under any voluntary system. Only adult descendants, young and able to work and to earn the few rupees that maintain life, can keep their parents from the fate of the old men who draw the death carts of India.

No people, even if trained to stoicism by generations of agony or conditioned by a religion of nonviolence, will endure such conditions forever—particularly if conditions worsen, as they have been doing since the rise in the price of oil. Only oil products from abroad enable India to fertilize her pitifully barren fields. Already stripped of foreign exchange, India simply cannot pay the extortionate price. While the oil sheiks become billionaires, India and vast stretches of Africa become more and more the ghettos of the world, with lepers, beggars, and the dying infesting the streets. How long will it be before the psychology of laceration with its accompanying terrorism takes root here? World science is now such that anyone courageous or desperate enough to steal the necessary elements can make an atom bomb small enough to be concealed in an ordinary package. How long before the starving of our world begin to apply terroristic blackmail to the affluent of our world? And who can blame them if they do? The suffering of the innocent is the great well of terrorism in our time, and that well has only begun to send out from its endless depths the floods certain to come.

Laceration is all but impossible to contain once it has begun. The modes of applying pressure which are emphatically nonviolent are sometimes the most damaging to those being pressured. The harsh spiritual blackmail that draws universal sympathy is stronger than the violence of, for example, putting obdurately self-publicizing dissenters into lunatic asylums. Because of the nonviolent laceration used against it, Russia has lost enormously in the prestige it once enjoyed. Russia's case is particularly significant because it shows that even the most rigid repression is helpless against laceration. Modern Russian methods of repression make those of the Tsars seem mild, yet Solzhenitsyn and those Russian dissidents who to a lesser degree follow his example are extremely effective as practitioners of laceration. Solzhenitsyn in his first book spoke for millions of prisoners and former prisoners like himself; he spoke for all people crushed and wronged by Russian totalitarianism. After the official publication of *One Day in the Life of Ivan Denisovich* and his recognition by Khrushchev, Solzhenitsyn could have absolved Russia of the wrongs done to him and to millions of others by settling down into a role of honor and prestige within the Soviet establishment. Instead he refused to give up his advantages as unforgiving man wronged. These advantages he wanted not so much for himself as for use on behalf of the unseen millions at the bottom of the Russian ant heap. He rejected the place of honor and conformity open to him, and not only insisted on his identity as a human being wronged but forced the reluctant Russian state to continue to wrong him, to continue publicly to lacerate him, and in the familiar pattern of laceration, each wrong only increased his identity and his power. By publishing *First Circle* and *Cancer Ward*, underground in Russia and openly abroad (the former a novel that used the concentration camp as a metaphor for all of Russia seen as a gigantic prison, the latter similarly a metaphor for Russia as a nation universally infected with cancer and run like a gigantic hospital), Solzhenitsyn gave the Russian authorities no choice but to wrong him still further by attacking him, threatening him, and banning his works. Almost single-handedly Solzhenitsyn by thus forcing Russia to give him the public identity of lacerated man brought the enormous Russian bureaucracy to such a pitch of frantic assertion of its own innocence that it had no alternative before the eyes of the watching world but to let Solzhenitsyn go free, to exile him. Solzhenitsyn, who loved his country, rightly claimed this as the greatest laceration of all— thus undoing at a stroke the claim of innocence that the Russian authorities had been working so hard to establish.

Laceration has its power only because of the capacity of human beings to feel shame and guilt. The growing use of laceration indicates that in the last hundred years the power of shame and guilt, far from declining, has increased. If, as has been often said, the one demonstrable theological truth may be original sin, then we have in mid-twentieth century a scramble for fig leaves which has seldom been equaled in history. Modern communications make shameful situations harder than ever to conceal. The efforts to conceal them have increased accordingly.

On the other hand, laceration is a psychological perversion that involves the most complex deceit and self-deceit. It spawns violence and terror. It confuses particular guilt with universal guilt. The lacerated person has a vision in which guilt and innocence are so inextricably mixed that the very terms become meaningless.

A strange thing, therefore, is happening. Shame and guilt are afflicting the human consciousness to a degree astonishing in a species that has had so many excellent opportunities to harden itself. At the same time the techniques of creating feelings of shame and guilt attack the very distinction between guilt and innocence that makes the reflexes of shame and guilt possible. It is a spectacle of opposites functioning in a simultaneity that most people would reasonably conclude to be impossible to maintain. Yet obviously this simultaneity has been and is continuing.

It was tragically inevitable that Russia, where laceration was first diagnosed, should suffer so conspicuously from laceration a century later. Solzhenitsyn and those Russians like him are the most appealing of modern individual sufferers. It was also in Russia a century ago that the most striking proposals were made for remedying the conditions that caused laceration. Russia, the first of the great modern ant heaps in the West, was the nation of Dostoevsky's Ivan Karamazov and Father Zossima. Obsessed by the human suffering in their time, they were diametrically opposite in the solutions they proposed. When Dostoevsky's novel was coming out in installments in the eighteen-seventies, thousands of readers were seizing each issue. Since that time, millions have become fascinated by the dilemma Dostoevsky presented. For this fascination there is good reason. The situations and the characters Dostoevsky portrayed were foreshadowings not only of what has since come to pass but of what many feel is even now still to be fulfilled in the world of the future as we see it shaping around us.

CHAPTER III

The Opposite Predictions
Ivan and Zossima

Dostoevsky gave only one book of his vast twelve-book epic explicitly to "laceration." The remainder of the novel rested on interaction between the two responses that he envisioned would be evoked by the challenges of ant heap existence. Dostoevsky so convincingly depicted and dramatized each of the two responses—that of Ivan the metaphysical rebel and that of Father Zossima the believer —that one can only conclude, as most critics do, that the two conflicted in Dostoevsky's own mind. He surely hoped for realization of the answer of Father Zossima, but the answer of Ivan may often in his life have seemed to him equally if not more probable.

The book's structure gave a large role to Ivan. Dostoevsky's plot depended on the working out of a parricide. All four brothers were shown in the end to have been in some way responsible for their father's death. But the central guilt rested on Ivan. Even if he did not strike the blow, he created the situation that led to it. Some reminder of how the plot proceeds is needed.

Dostoevsky's portrait of old Fyodor Karamazov, father of the four brothers, while highly individualized was also in effect a portrait of a type common in that time and place. Old Karamazov had no faith in either natural or supernatural order, and certainly none in Christianity. "Good Lord! to think what faith, what force of all kinds man has lavished for nothing, on that dream, and for how many thousand years."[1] Fyodor Karamazov lived as many skeptics did in the nineteenth century. He made as much money and enjoyed as much sensual satisfaction as possible. At the same time, however, enough of the old theological and moral frameworks remained in his consciousness to give him contempt for himself. To comfort himself for that contempt and the contempt of his neighbors, he indulged in a shameless, sniggering buffoonery by which he invited scorn in order to flout it, perversely delighting in it as a demonstration of his own superior scorn for others and for himself. As he told Father Zossima, "When you said just now, 'Don't be so ashamed of yourself for that is at the root of it all,' you pierced right through me by that remark, and read me to the core. Indeed, I always feel when I meet people that I am lower than all, and that they take me for a buffoon. So I say, 'Let me really play the buffoon. I am not afraid of your opinion, for you are every one of you worse than I am.' " Then, having spoken the truth, old Fyodor indicated his scorn for truth and for that speaker of truths,

Father Zossima, by clownishly flopping down on his knees and exclaiming, "Teacher! . . . what must I do to gain eternal life?"[2] He did not believe, but he had a remnant of the longing to believe, and he mocked that too. This was the man Dostoevsky made the father of the four Karamazov brothers: Dmitri, the man of passions, a "Demeter man," an earth man; Ivan, the intellectual; Smerdyakov, the criminal; and Alyosha, the "man of God," named for Russia's beloved Saint Alexey, who in legend was a holy man of the early Christian centuries. As the four represented four types in the humanity of their time and made up, so to speak, the "human family" of mid-nineteenth-century Russia, so old Fyodor, who spawned the four, represented the "father" of his era, unbelieving yet not quite unbelieving, but in his actions oriented entirely by greed and satisfaction of the senses. He assumed of course no responsibility toward his children, and in his scornful buffoonery flaunted that fact. In the case of the eldest, Dmitri, he even managed to embezzle much of Dmitri's inheritance. When Dmitri came to town to square accounts, old Fyodor began a campaign aimed at the seduction of Dmitri's beloved, the unpredictable Grushenka.

Dmitri was the most financially wronged of Fyodor Karamazov's four sons. But the youngest son, Smerdyakov, Fyodor's peasant bastard (whom Fyodor had trained to be his cook in the traditional servant role of Russian peasant to Russian elite), was a close second to Dmitri in having reason to hate his father. Smerdyakov's mother, a feeble-minded village vagabond, fed and protected by the villagers as one afflicted by God, was raped by Fyodor on a bet with some drunken companions. When her time came, the unfortunate mute woman climbed Fyodor's fence to deliver her child within his grounds. Because the mother's village nickname was Liza Smerdyakova, meaning "Stinking Liza," Fyodor's bastard was called by his father and everyone else simply "Smerdyakov" or "Stinky."

Smerdyakov grew up to be a brute, but a fastidious brute, one with intellectual aspirations. He played the guitar, inspected his food for flies before eating it, and confounded Fyodor's pious old manservant Grigory by refusing to absorb the Russian peasant's simple catechism. With a cunning that delighted old Fyodor and outraged Grigory, Smerdyakov demanded, "God created light on the first day, and the sun, moon, and stars on the fourth day. Where did the light come from on the first day?"[3]

Smerdyakov was given to vanity, passionless courtship of a passionless girl, and wordless brooding.[4] Dostoevsky's narrator said of Smerdyakov that he was a "contemplative" who spent most of his early years "greedily hoarding up his impressions" until the moment when they would explode into unaccountable or violent action.[5] As Dostoevsky caused Smerdyakov's half brother Ivan to observe, Smerdyakov was "raw material for revolution when the time comes."[6] The wronged and brooding peasant meanwhile formed a curious and invisible alliance with the cold and intellectual Ivan. When this alliance was formed, the plot which would lead to parricide began to move. Ivan's chief intellectual thesis was that "if God does not exist, everything is permitted," a concept that acted on Smerdyakov like a revelation.

Smerdyakov informed Ivan that Dmitri, who was watching his father's house for the coming of Grushenka, had been told by Smerdyakov that the signal old Fyodor had appointed for Smerdyakov to give if Grushenka arrived was to knock five times on the old man's door or garden window. The slyly clever Smerdyakov realized that the maddened Dmitri need only himself give the five knocks when the house was empty, gain entrance, and kill the old man, who was not only trying to buy Grushenka but had under his pillow the packet for her, containing precisely the three thousand rubles Dmitri had to have in order to repay Katya and which he considered rightfully his.

"Why don't you go to Tchermashnya, sir?" Smerdyakov asked Ivan.[7] Tchermashnya or Black Forest was the name of the town old Fyodor had been asking Ivan to go to in order to collect three thousand rubles for the senior Karamazov's real estate speculations. (Black Forest was also the name of the town in which Dostoevsky's own father had been murdered.)

Ivan hesitated to go to Tchermashnya, not consciously aware of any reasons for delay but remaining for some time in a state of procrastination. Finally he announced that he would go, his father having asked him even more urgently. " 'You force me to go to that damned Tchermashnya yourself, then?' cried Ivan, with a malignant smile."[8] Smerdyakov obsequiously tucked the rug around Ivan's knees in the carriage that was to take him away. " 'You see . . . I am going to Tchermashnya,' broke suddenly from Ivan." And Smerdyakov replied, " 'It's a true saying then, that "it's always worth while speaking to a clever man." ' "[9]

Ivan went not to Tchermashnya but to Moscow, a change that in no way altered the fact that the house with old Fyodor in it was now open to Dmitri's entry. That night Dmitri did break into the grounds. But Dmitri Karamazov was a man of passion and open violence, not murder by stealth. He did knock Grigory senseless as he leaped back over the wall but he did not kill his father. That was done later by Smerdyakov, who seized the three thousand rubles.

In the course of Dmitri's trial Dostoevsky demonstrated an astonishing truth: Ivan had been absolutely unaware of his role in the parricide. He believed sincerely that his brother Dmitri was the murderer. This aspect of the plot is typical of every alliance between intellectual and brute from the time of Robespierre and the Paris mob to Hitler and his brownshirts. In this pattern the theorist establishes the principle which the brute carries out and each is convinced of his own righteousness. This is so obscure to many readers of *The Brothers Karamazov* that they do not grasp Ivan's obliviousness at all until the next to the last book, when Ivan, during three interviews with Smerdyakov, becomes aware of what their relationship has actually been. To his utter astonishment, Ivan discovered that Smerdyakov believed that it was Ivan who first taught him the ideology according to which the old man could be killed and Dmitri set up as the murderer when he said, "If God does not exist, everything is permitted." He believed that Ivan had given the signal to put the plan in motion by leaving the Karamazov house empty—"I am going to Tchermashnya." The two Karamazovs, Ivan the intellectual and Smerdyakov the killer, had worked together in a psychological alliance whose effect was to absolve each of conscious responsibility. The barrier Ivan maintained between his actions and his awareness of their consequences kept him from having any knowing share in the parricide. The assurance Smerdyakov had from Ivan that "everything is permitted" had licensed him to kill without responsibility, for the world as portrayed to him by Ivan, made such an action perfectly logical. When Smerdyakov discovered that Ivan had been unaware of the fruits of his teachings and had given no conscious signal by his announcement about going to Tchermashnya, Smerdyakov was unable to bear the disintegration of the bond of brotherhood with his leader and the consequent collapse of his world into chaos. He killed himself. Meanwhile recognition of his own guilt drove Ivan to insanity.

Ivan had never met himself, did not know himself, had no recognition of the evil that had entered him through his unconscious. In his final insane confrontation with the facts about himself, he believed he was in conversation with the devil. For Dostoevsky there were always three levels on which human beings acted: the situational, the psychological, and the metaphysical. Metaphysical evil, the evil principle itself, entered Ivan through his unconscious, through his psychological estrangement from his true self and so from all accurate self-knowledge. The metaphysical and the psychological levels of Ivan's being created on the situational level the circumstances that made Ivan, not Dmitri or even Smerdyakov, most completely their father's murderer. Dmitri's raging passions provided the opportunity, Smerdyakov's criminality struck the blow, but Ivan's theorizing made the entire situation possible, for "everything is permitted" had also influenced Dmitri.[10] Of all the brothers, only Alyosha, the man of God, seemed by the book's end to have had no share in the parricide that Dostoevsky saw as a symbol of man's overturn of moral order. Nevertheless, it would seem that there are good grounds for questioning even the complete innocence of the man of God, if Dostoevsky's parable of the human condition in the Russia of his time is regarded as accurate.

Alyosha's "guilt," if one could call it that, began to be visible quite early, in Book V, Chapter III, "The Brothers Make Friends." In an upper room in an inn, Ivan prepared to tell Alyosha his "poem," "The Legend of the Grand Inquisitor," which was to become one of the most famous pieces of symbolic literature of all time. Early during the two years that the wide audience of *The Brothers Karamazov* was reading the novel as it came out in installments, Dostoevsky himself realized how strong would be the impact of "The Legend." Dostoevsky's own vulnerability to it, and his confidence in his power to overcome it, are both indicated in a letter he wrote at the time to his aristocratic and conservative friend, Konstantin Pobedonostsev,[11] adviser to the Tsar and Procurator of the Holy Synod: "This book is the culmination of my novel and is called *Pro and Contra*. Its meaning is the following: blasphemy and its answer. The blasphemy is already finished and sent in; I'll send the answer in July."[12] Formulation of the "answer" was not to be as simple as Dostoevsky in his letter seemed to believe. Almost all the rest of the novel is concerned somehow with developing the "answer."

Ivan began by establishing laceration over his brother. He prefaced the legend by telling Alyosha first a medieval fable about the Mother of God's voyage through hell, where she saw the torments of the damned and implored God for a respite. He followed this with three stories of children on earth who were tortured by adults. He then told Alyosha that while he, Ivan Karamazov, did not disbelieve in God, he found the entrance price to God's world too high and had decided that he would "most respectfully return him the ticket."[13] What Ivan was saying was that he could not endure to contemplate either the fate of the damned after death or the suffering of children on earth. Thus Alyosha, as a monk and so a person who consented to accept God's creation, had a harder heart than Ivan's and was inferior both in his own suffering and in his empathy for the sufferings of others.

Ivan's three stories of child abuse were historically accurate. Dostoevsky was constantly culling books and newspapers for such accounts. He himself was never more touched than by children. The death of his own little son Alexey shortly before he began to write *The Brothers Karamazov* so affected Dostoevsky that he spent the entire night praying beside the dead child's crib. His wife, Anya, persuaded him to go to a famous monastery and seek counsel from its elder, Father Amvrosy. It was Father Amvrosy's words of consolation that Dostoevsky gave to Father Zossima, when Zossima spoke to the mother of a dead child in the beginning of the novel.[14] Alyosha bears the name of Dostoevsky's dead child, Alexey, named after the "man of God" who lived unknown in the world, as Father Zossima was to require Alyosha to live. Even before the ending of Alyosha's apprenticeship in the monastery, Father Zossima, the spiritual father of Alyosha as Fyodor was Alyosha's physical father, was constantly sending Alyosha out to seek and serve his brethren.

Alyosha was actually looking for Dmitri when Ivan leaned out the window at the inn and called to him. After they sat down together and Ivan had duly established his dominance as "sufferer," Ivan revealed his "poem." It was a story of Catholic Spain, with all the villainy Catholics, as founders of a spiritual political kingdom, had historically symbolized to Russians. In sixteenth-century Seville, where the Grand Inquisitor has just burned alive almost a hundred heretics, Christ returns to earth. His peaceful face, his divine gentleness would prove who he is even if he did not repeat his miracle of "Maiden, arise." A little girl, at his compassionate word, sits up in her coffin and is restored to her rejoicing family. At that moment the Grand Inquisitor arrives and also recognizes Christ. The Inquisitor "holds out his finger and bids the guards take him."[15] There is no doubt whose power over the people is greater, the power of Christ or the power of the Grand Inquisitor. The people fall back, the soldiers seize Christ, and God himself is imprisoned in the dungeons of the Inquisition.

Here the Inquisitor comes to interrogate his prisoner. Since Christ does not speak, the interview consists entirely of the Grand Inquisitor's justification. Sixteen hundred years ago, the Grand Inquisitor says, when the "Great Spirit" came to Christ in the wilderness, Christ refused the only course that would have made humanity's life on earth bearable. He refused to turn stones into bread, to cast himself down from the temple and prove his divinity, or to adore the Great Spirit, the principle of earthly power. Had Christ hearkened to the Great Spirit, Christ would have established forever an undisputed reign of mystery, miracle, and authority. Instead he left the people free to believe or not to believe. Christ thus stands indicted by history, says the Grand Inquisitor, for of all the human beings who have been born since Christ's refusal of the Great Spirit's call for visible proof, only a handful have had the strength to follow freely the teachings of Christ. "Feed men and then ask of them virtue!" exclaims the Inquisitor.[16] The burden of freedom as Christ imposed it is beyond the strength of ordinary mortals. The Grand Inquisitor himself fasted in the wilderness. He longed for the impossible acceptance. Now he knows better.

Freedom, says the Grand Inquisitor, is the greatest of evils. Freedom makes men responsible for what they do. (This claim carried out Ivan's theme of the children tortured by human brutality.) Freedom is the burden from which man most desires to be delivered. The Grand Inquisitor and the elite to which he belongs have had mercy on the people. They have accepted from the people the terrible burden that the people have rushed to lay down. They alone know now the fearful secret that man is free. And, relieved of freedom, the people live in happy innocence. (The context of Ivan's poem makes almost invisible the point that every so often some of these "happy" people have to be burned alive to prevent revolt against the regime. Clearly that fact does not disturb the contentment of the majority.)

From the time of "The Legend's" publication, the ending of the story, which described the reaction of Christ, stirred the deepest emotion. "The old man longed for Him to say something, however bitter and terrible. But He suddenly approached the old man in silence and softly kissed him on his bloodless aged lips. That was all his answer."[17] Shuddering, the Grand Inquisitor opens the door. Christ glides silently away.

The German theologian, Romano Guardini, said in 1954 that the Christ of the "Legend" was not the Christ of the gospels but the Christ envisioned by Ivan Karamazov, whose views he reflected. "The Christ of the Grand Inquisitor . . . does not accept the order of the world. He has no essential relationship with the Father-Creator. He is not truly the Word, in whom the world has been created, and whose incarnation ought to regenerate it by transforming it. This Christ does not have that holy relationship of love for the real world which purifies it and renews it; he is simply compassion, bearing an invitation to leave the world."[18] If, as Guardini claimed, Ivan's Christ failed by being simply "compassion," perhaps Alyosha also somehow repeated that failure. When Ivan asked Alyosha for a reply to the "Legend," Alyosha rose and in silence kissed him before quietly leaving—an end to the interview which the delighted Ivan hailed as "plagiarism." It was then that Ivan went home and the die of his fate was cast as he allowed himself to be persuaded by Smerdyakov to go to Tchermashnya.

If Ivan, by opening his innermost thoughts to Alyosha, was unconsciously asking for help, if he obscurely expected that the man of God would be able to still the revolt and alter the activities of Ivan Karamazov, then the Karamazov brother in whom Dostoevsky depicted the man of God failed him. And, whether Dostoevsky liked it or not, this must have been the truth as he saw it, since he used the silent answer twice: once with Ivan's Christ and once with Alyosha. The fact may have been simply that Ivan, particularly by the laceration he had used as a prelude to his "Legend," had cut himself off so completely from his brother that Alyosha could not in any more positive manner have reached him. Ivan, who said that one "can love one's neighbors in the abstract, or even at a distance, but at close quarters it's almost impossible,"[19] had the alienated person's craving for solidarity, but it was not the solidarity of the heart. What Ivan craved was the solidarity described by the Inquisitor, the political-social solidarity of a dictatorial regime backed by what the psychologist Erich Fromm calls the "escape from freedom,"[20] the complex of the modern era. Thus Dostoevsky, who called "The Legend" and its prelude "this blasphemy" and said he had taken it in its "strongest form" as it was current in his time, had also delineated at least the quality of what he saw as the "answer" long before the Zossima section in which the answer was actually set forth. It was to be an answer of love and acceptance, but perhaps also one that could not change the truly alienated like Ivan. If so, it is no wonder that many of Dostoevsky's readers then and now, and perhaps Dostoevsky himself, felt troubled by the "answer." Although the answer is persuasive, it clearly cannot reach the people it most needs to reach: the blind and alienated Ivan Karamazovs.

In the section in which Dostoevsky developed his answer, Father Zossima is dying. He assembles the monks around him. As Ivan did, he tells three stories. The first concerns Zossima's boyhood memories of his brother Markel who, when facing death from tuberculosis, underwent a conversion from complete unbelief to a sense of mystical union with all the universe. Markel said that if we knew the truth we would ask "pardon" even of the birds for our lack of love for the beings around us. "We are all in paradise, but we won't see it; if we would we should have heaven on earth the next day."[21] Years later Zossima, then a young army officer, recalling Markel's story, aborted a murderous duel to which he had challenged a successful rival in love. Zossima stood to receive his opponent's fire, then threw his own gun away. As a result of Zossima's action, a murderer came to confess to him and later publicly acknowledged the guilt of an undetected crime.

One thing Dostoevsky was doing in Father Zossima's three stories was illustrating Zossima's central contention that humanity is like an ocean: all is flowing and blending; a touch in one place sets up movement at the other end of the earth,[22] so that in this sensitive human sea "each is responsible for all."[23] Father Zossima's stories showed a living chain of altered lives. The murderer's life was changed by Zossima's action at his duel. Zossima's action at his duel was caused by memory of his brother Markel's experience of mystical human solidarity.

Dostoevsky then developed a second demonstration of human encounter and the solidarity of living chains of "each is responsible for all." He portrayed a meeting between Alyosha and Grushenka, in which Alyosha recovered his faith, nearly shattered after Father Zossima's death, and Grushenka gave up her vindictiveness against a world in which she had been seduced, exploited, and abandoned. The book from then on became full of such living chains. Zossima, Alyosha, and Grushenka were one chain. Another was Alyosha, Ilusha, and Ilusha's persecutor, an extraordinary schoolboy named Kolya, whose orientation Alyosha changed from self-centeredness to empathy. Other chains continued to the very last words of the novel which told of Alyosha with the schoolboys, Dostoevsky's man of God with the next Russian generation.

So a portrayal of the human sea in which living currents from person to person carried the good was what Dostoevsky counterpointed as answer to Ivan's "Legend." Against the "Legend's" political, social, and psychological solidarity, Dostoevsky set a metaphysical solidarity. In the solidarity of Ivan's "Legend," freedom was given up. The human sea, on the contrary, was composed of autonomous individuals. Grushenka had to *decide* whether or not to forgive her seducer. Dmitri had to decide whether or not to accept without bitterness the conviction for a murder he did not commit. Ivan's "Legend" showed man abdicating responsibility, as Ivan abdicated it to Smerdyakov and Smerdyakov abdicated it to Ivan. In reply, the remainder of Dostoevsky's masterpiece was orchestrated to show hundreds of individual decisions in a human sea that stirred at every touch, sending out ripples to the very limits of humanity. In that sea the battle between alienation and solidarity ceased. No one is alienated from his fellows because, if each person is responsible for every other person, then every life is open to every other life for each person who recognizes the truth.

If one thing Dostoevsky was doing in portraying the human sea was to illustrate what he believed was the only viable relationship between human beings, the other was to illustrate what he believed to be the relationship between man and the Life Force behind the universe. It is lack of recognition of Dostoevsky's Russian and Byzantine background rather than hostility to the metaphysical per se that now keeps so much of this part of his vision unseen. The Eastern Fathers of the Byzantine Church, from the time of Irenaeus and Cyril, had regarded Christ as Pantocrator, reigning forever in the golden light of that holy mission expressed by the Byzantine mosaics and carried into Russian sacred painting. Under Christ Pantocrator all the human race was divinized. The very ground was sacred. Dostoevsky has Alyosha reverently kiss the earth to mark his reconciliation with his faith after Father Zossima's death. To the Russian mind the concept expressed in Western religious painting, from the earliest times right through the Renaissance, of an earth which remained "earthly," while rays from heaven falling on Christ, the Virgin, or the saints symbolized the power sent forth by heaven to redeem man from sin, was utterly unassimilable. To the West, the Russian concept of a sacred earth was equally foreign. Until the very recent time of spontaneous recognition in the West of the sacred earth—the recognition expressed, for example, by the work of Teilhard de Chardin and his followers —most of the metaphysical coloring of Dostoevsky's vision was carried almost without comprehension into Europe by other visionaries he influenced. One doubts if Camus, for instance, who read Dostoevsky so earnestly, recognized the metaphysical connotations embedded in the passages that showed his own reverence for sea and earth preexisting in Alyosha and even in Ivan, who loved the "little sticky leaves."[24] The fact that this part of Russian thought which came into the West with the enthusiasm for Dostoevsky was not understood as metaphysical perhaps made it more able to penetrate non-Russian thinking. Because the metaphysical elements were not overtly visible to those who passed them on, these elements did not arouse resistance from a period that tended to oppose metaphysical consciousness of whatever kind, a period of intolerance which we now seem fortunately to be leaving behind.

Markel's influence on Zossima depended on Zossima's reactions at a time when Zossima's life was such as to dishonor Markel's memory. So far Dostoevsky's portrayal of the sea from Markel to Zossima was situational and psychological. Markel, however, was the first ripple and, with Markel, Dostoevsky fell back entirely on the metaphysical and the sacred. Markel at seventeen was a young unbeliever, whose atheism had been shaped by his encounter with a freethinking, revolutionary political exile. When Markel's fatal illness was diagnosed, he went to church to please his mother. He later confessed and received the sacrament. After that his view of life changed. This change was simply and obviously, as Dostoevsky portrayed it, the effect of supernatural grace, a participation in the life of God that showed God's sacred earth as it actually was. Thus the direct initiative from God was the beginning of the stirring in the human sea. To Markel after his conversion the earth was a "paradise." He felt that all people, if their consciousness were not obscured, would recognize the truth and, as he said, "have heaven on earth the next day." This was the ancient Byzantine vision. Earth was paradise and humanity was directly and forever in God's golden light. Together with this vision, and almost as old, was the Russian sense of humanity's betrayal. Blinded Russia had enslaved God's holy people. Blinded Russia had treasonably turned away from the sacred reign of Christ Pantocrator. That Russia had betrayed a mission was expressed by Pushkin, Lermontov, Gogol, and Tolstoy. It is, for that matter, also expressed by Solzhenitsyn. Dostoevsky, however, drew the most vividly metaphysical of the portraits of betrayal. What Dostoevsky conveyed in the Markel section of *The Brothers Karamazov*, and in an extraodinary short story written a year earlier, "The Dream of a Ridiculous Man," was that the actual nature of the earth was such that if only all would consent to receive God's grace as Markel did, all could see the truth: God had set man in paradise. It would suffice for man to cease from sinning, the lion would lie down with the lamb, and humanity would be wedded to the gentle Christ, "awful in his sublimity, but infinitely merciful."[25]

It was a vision of Byzantine glory. It contained, however, the most uncompromising indictment of human responsibility. The human race, left free by its Creator, had wronged the noble Word of God that uttered the universe. The realization of paradise on earth was therefore removed to the remote future. Alyosha was the type of that future, but humanity was not with him. Dostoevsky said of Alyosha that his "hero" carried "within himself the very heart of the universal, and the rest of the men of his epoch have for some reason been temporarily torn from it, as if by a gust of wind . . ."[26]

If often in the novel Alyosha did not seem to be a fully developed character, perhaps one reason was that Dostoevsky could see him only as a person who was to come into being in the future, when Markel's and Zossima's vision of the truth of paradise on earth might be recognized.[27] It may have been that Dostoevsky did not show the person of the future more clearly because he felt that in his own time such people were only foreshadowed. They had not yet come fully into existence. There is something ghostlike about Alyosha. It is as if a figure sketched on Dostoevsky's canvas had not been quite filled in.

Who was filled in on Dostoevsky's canvas was Alyosha's opposite, old Fyodor Karamazov. Utterly separated from his fellow creatures, separated even from himself, he had no understanding of his own nature, of what he believed, or of why he acted as he did. Fyodor was a further stage in the development of the Russian type of alienated personality depicted by Gogol and Lermontov. Dostoevsky saw such alienation as an ongoing condition. Of the Russia in his own day Dostoevsky had Father Zossima say:

". . . the isolation that prevails everywhere, above all in our age . . . has not fully developed, it has not reached its limit yet. For every one strives to keep his individuality as apart as possible, wishes to secure the greatest possible fullness of life

for himself, but meantime all his efforts result not in attain-
ing fullness of life but in self-destruction, for instead of self-
realization he ends by arriving at complete solitude. All
mankind in our age have split up into units, they all keep
apart, each in his own groove: each one holds aloof, hides
himself and hides what he has, from the rest, and he ends up
by being repelled by others and repelling them."[28]

It is significant that Dostoevsky made this vision of humanity as a mass of mutually repellent particles part of
Zossima's thought. Zossima, unlike Ivan, was a reliable
narrator, a character into whose words Dostoevsky put the
truth as he himself saw it. Even Zossima, who described the
human sea as the shape of the future, saw an opposite
shape growing against it: an enmity of all against all, an
estrangement of every person from every other, so that the
most developed pattern of estrangement in Dostoevsky's
novel, Ivan, far surpassed his father in psychological solitude, and in his alliance with Smerdyakov did not even
know what he or his ally were doing.

Three months after the completion of *The Brothers
Karamazov*, Dostoevsky lay dying. The novel had been received with enormous enthusiasm. The first bound copy
had been presented to the crown prince. The night before
he died Dostoevsky asked Anya to read to their children
the parable of the Prodigal Son. There can be no doubt that
he saw as universal the pattern he believed that he himself
had followed. He was a rebel who had come home to his
fatherland, to his Tsar, and to God. But at Dostoevsky's
funeral, among the delegations that made up the reverent
procession of thirty thousand people, was a band of stu-

dents carrying the leg-irons of a prisoner in Siberia. Which was the real Dostoevsky? The rebel he once was and whom he portrayed in Ivan? The man of passion he also was and portrayed in Dmitri? The man of God, Alyosha? The pathological Smerdyakov, who shared Dostoevsky's affliction of epilepsy? A friend, after his death, did not hesitate to accuse him of inhuman acts, specifically the rape of a child.[29] In any case it was fitting that Dostoevsky should have been not only a man of complex contradictions but also of puzzles never solved. He was the first of the prophetic writers to attract an immense and concerned audience to consider the conflict between alienation and solidarity. His prophecy was clear. Solidarity would prevail. But which solidarity? The beneficent human sea envisioned by Father Zossima? Or the iron rule of Ivan's creature, the Grand Inquisitor, who turned politics into religion, as Hitler was to do with the blood and soil creed of the Third Reich, as Stalin was to do with his version of the teachings of Marx, and as China was to do with the "little red book" that sacramentalized "the thought" of Mao?

Dostoevsky saw the prophecies of Ivan and Zossima as mutually exclusive. If one developed, the other could not. As Dostoevsky shaped his novel, he was trying to tell his nation and the world the truth about itself. Humanity, as he saw it, was torn between opposing alternatives. On the choice of one or the other would depend the future of the race. It remains to see how far Dostoevsky was regarded by later prophetic writers as having been correct in this book, which has been regarded with such reverence that T. E. Lawrence called it the "Fifth Gospel."

CHAPTER IV

Simultaneity of Opposites
Jean-Paul Sartre

Never did a nation more need a prophetic writer to tell it about itself than did France during the Second World War. Jean-Paul Sartre, philosopher, dramatist, novelist, teacher, former prisoner of war and counselor to the French resistance, filled that role. Many who experienced the attraction of the savant of the Café de Flore remained under his influence for the rest of their lives. Between 1935 and 1960 the voice of Sartre became one of the most widely heeded in the Western world.

His message was beguiling. The famous anecdote he himself told to illustrate his application of his form of existialism to the lives of young Frenchmen under the German occupation was as appealing as any passage in the literature of modern times.

... a pupil of mine sought me out in the following circumstances. His father was quarreling with his mother and was
also inclined to be a "collaborator," his elder brother had
been killed in the German offensive of 1940 and this young
man, with a sentiment somewhat primitive but generous,
burned to avenge him. . . . But he . . . had the choice between
going to England to join the Free French Forces or staying
near his mother . . . he was hesitating between two kinds of
morality: on the one side the morality of sympathy, of personal devotion, and on the other side, a morality of wider
scope. . . . I had but one reply to make. You are free, therefore choose—that is to say, invent. No rule of general morality can show you what you ought to do. . . .[1]

According to this counsel each person made his own life—
alone and without recourse. The merit of Sartre in the anecdote was that he did not advise. He taught freedom and
the necessity of choice as escape from the anguish of alternate possibilities. Anguish, as Sartre's predecessor Kierke-
gaard had seen a century earlier, came from the modern
fragmentation, in which the traditions of religion, nation,
family, and class no longer told one what had precedence
or what to do, and the individual was cast on his own.

In the same lecture as the one in 1946 in which Sartre
had told the anecdote of the young man, a lecture given for
the benefit of the many who had heard of Sartre but who
found his massive book *Being and Nothingness* published
in 1943 too difficult to read, Sartre disclosed that his basic
premise was Ivan Karamazov's thesis, "If God does not
exist, everything is permitted." Atheism, which in the modern world had normally given rise to despair, was made in
Sartre's existentialism a foundation of hope. The portrait

Sartre gave of man, of the individual in *Being and Nothingness*, was of a moving point constantly advancing into new self-creation, for if there was no God to conceive human nature a priori, existence preceded essence and each person made his own essence, as the moving point, which was himself, advanced from past into future. According to Sartre, the past was a has-been which man, the moving point, left behind. The future was a not-yet toward which man moved in constant pursuit of an actuality which became past as rapidly as he overtook it. Man was nothingness continually coming into being. Descartes was wrong to say, "I think, therefore I am." He should have said, "I thought, therefore I was," because by the time he articulated the thought the moment had already gone. Radical change was thus part of man's nature. A man who took human life (perhaps he killed a Nazi) and saw his act as murder as he plunged in the knife, might see it as an act of liberation if the man the Nazi had been holding prisoner ran away safely beside his rescuer. The murderer had been transformed into a patriot. As a patriot he rushed into the future to maintain his essence by performing constantly new acts of patriotism, while the future as constantly eluded him as each act in succession was transformed into past, leaving him always with the necessity of redefining his ongoing essence.

Well known though the vision is, it is well to recall it, particularly the context of commitment to patriotism and the freeing of the human race which marked it during the resistance. To understand the role of Sartre one must bear in mind two things: his ineradicable sense of mission, which was the outgrowth of his experiences during the occupation, and the sense of life as a perpetual advance into a perpetually elusive future. Sartre continually left his own past behind and shaped himself anew, so that bewilderingly there would eventually seem to have been not one but many Sartres. Even as I write, and as you read, a new Sartre is coming into being. And so, he believes, it must be with all of us. Only by constantly recalling this fact can one see Sartre as what, paradoxically, he is: one of the most consistent voices in the West.

The origins of Sartre's thought are in metaphysics, particularly in the metaphysical orientations current in the France of his time. Like many of his own existential heroes, he began as a metaphysical rebel. In the autobiography of his childhood, *The Words*, Sartre gives an account of his early experiences with religion. The passages are curious. They seem to be about not so much things that happened as things that did not happen.

Raised in the Catholic faith, I learned that the Almighty had made me for his glory. That was more than I dared dream. But later, I did not recognize in the fashionable God in whom I was taught to believe the One whom my soul was awaiting. I needed a Creator; I was given a Big Boss. The two were one and the same, but I didn't realize it. I was serving, without zeal, the Idol of the Pharisees, and the official doctrine put me off seeking my own faith. What luck! Confidence and sorrow made my soul a choice soil for sowing the seeds of heaven. Were it not for that mistake, I would now be a monk. But my family had been affected by the slow dechristianization that started among the Voltairean bourgeoisie and took a century to spread to all levels of society. . . . Good Society believed in God in order not to speak of him. How tolerant religion seemed! How comfortable it was: the Christian could desert the Mass and let his children marry in church, could smile at "all that holy stuff" and shed tears as he listened to the Wedding March from *Lohengrin*. He was not obliged either to lead an exemplary life or to die in a state of despair. . . .[2]

Jean-Paul was a pious little boy. According to him, the final break with God came when he handed in a school composition on the passion. It received "only the silver medal." After that: "For several years more, I maintained public relations with the Almighty. But privately I ceased to associate with him. Only once did I have the feeling that he existed. I had been playing with matches and burned a small rug. I was in the process of covering up my crime when suddenly God saw me. I felt his gaze inside my head and on my hands. I whirled about in the bathroom, horribly visible, a live target. Indignation saved me. I flew into a rage against so crude an indiscretion, I blasphemed, I muttered like my grandfather: 'God damn it, God damn it, God damn it.' He never looked at me again."

The thing that shines through this odd account is the "indignation." Something transpired that resembled a failed love affair—a relation to religion that affects many people in our time. "Whenever anyone speaks to me about him today, I say, with the easy amusement of an old beau who meets a former belle: 'Fifty years ago, had it not been for that misunderstanding, that mistake, the accident that separated us, there might have been something between us.' "[3]

Sartre had a naturally religious consciousness which in childhood found the religion of his time and place emotionally inadequate. In maturity he was to find it intellectually inadequate. I think he was profoundly affected by the vacuum, the "nothingness," he experienced where something should have been: "He never looked at me again." In any case, the religious condition of his post-"Voltairean bourgeoisie" shaped his thought. In Sartre's young manhood, neo-Thomism was officially the philosophy of Catholicism among the intellectuals of ostensibly Catholic France. Maritain and Gilson were attracting worldwide attention in those days of the Catholic renaissance. Sartre's own philosophy reverses the neo-Thomist philosophy—with precision and in detail. One may almost say that the reversal acts as the "springboard," so to speak, for Sartre's central premises. Saint Thomas, following Augustine, had drawn upon the Platonic theory of ideas. Thomas wrote: "Therefore Augustine for the ideas defended by Plato substituted the types of all creatures existing in the Divine mind, according to which types all things are made in themselves. . . ."[4] Here is Sartre's explanation of his most fundamental contention: that existence comes before essence. It is a precise opposite of the Catholic thought of his era. Sartre begins by saying that when a man makes a book or a paper knife he has in mind the design of that paper knife and what it will be used for. He then continues:

> When we think of God as the Creator, we are thinking of him, most of the time, as a Supernal Artisan. Whatever doctrine we may be considering, whether it be a doctrine like that of Descartes, or of Leibnitz himself, we always imply that the

will follows, more or less, from the understanding or at least accompanies it, so that when God creates he knows precisely what he is creating. Thus, the conception of man in the mind of God is comparable to that of the paper knife in the mind of the artisan: God makes man according to a procedure and a conception, exactly as the artisan manufactures a paper knife, following a definition and formula. . . .

Atheistic existentialism, of which I am a representative, declares with greater consistency that if God does not exist there is at least one being whose existence comes before its essence, a being which exists before it can be defined by any conception of it. That being is man or, as Heidegger has it, the human reality. What do we mean by saying that existence precedes essence? We mean that man first of all exists, encounters himself, surges up in the world—and defines himself afterwards. If man as the existentialist sees him is not definable, it is because to begin with he is nothing. He will not be anything until later, and then he will be what he makes of himself. Thus, there is no human nature, because there is no God to have conception of it.[5]

Thus, as Dostoevsky reflected the culture of Russia, so Sartre reflected the culture of France. It is impossible to understand the creation of his first play, *The Flies*, without taking into account the preponderant metaphysics of the French nation and the preponderant politics of the years that led up to 1943, when the German censors passed what they thought was a harmless antireligious drama by an atheistic young writer and found themselves with an epidemic of patriotic fervor on their hands.

Ever since the rise to power of Adolf Hitler in 1932, France had dreaded a repetition of her defeat by Germany in 1870. Particularly vocal were the French conservatives.

Although they had been out of power for decades, they were still a cultural force with slogans like "honor and France" and "God and Christian unity." These slogans were not only powerful among the scattered followers of Charles Maurras and Action Française, who lingered from the nineteen-twenties, but were also part of the living tissue of French thought during the next decade, a fact demonstrated by the popularity of such authors as the Catholic novelist Georges Bernanos. This type of ardent and sincere patriotism was especially strong among the clergy and in the officer corps, both of which habitually provided vocations for the sons of conservative families. The French government, from 1830 to the time of its surrender to the Nazis, was controlled by the bourgeoisie. This class by 1932 and the beginning of the rise of Hitler segmented into so many different kinds of political opinion that it is hard to state what all had in common except that they focused almost invariably on some form of material welfare for the French people. Rightist idealism had to do with defense of the country and emphasis on the duty of France, as embodying the tradition of "honneur" and "grandeur," to lead Europe's civilizing mission (the constellation of ideas that was later to inspire Gaullism). Middle-of-the-road bourgeois idealism and the idealism of the moderate left, which since the nineteen-hundreds had divided control of the government, was to improve the country's economic position. This aim included a wide range of objectives from increasing the productiveness of French industry to clearing the slums, a program made more urgent by the far left's agitation for a Marxist France.

The quarrel centered on what disposition to make of the nation's limited revenues. The officer corps wanted arms and pointed to the Nazi danger. This plea was also taken up by many Catholics, who saw in Hitler an incarnation of the evil principle, anti-Christian, monstrously brutal, and avowedly pagan. The governments on the other hand—so many rose and fell that one must speak of them in the plural—wanted material progress and social amelioration and pointed to the compelling needs of the unemployed and the hardships of the poor. According to the leaders of these governments, France simply had no money to spend on the army. In any case, there would not be a war. Conciliation of Germany would see to that. Besides, the Maginot Line was impregnable, as Hitler knew. So it was said, and so most Frenchmen believed.

When the German panzers overran France, the French right bitterly saw its predictions come true. In their view France had transgressed against honor and her own greatness, and France was being justly punished. The spirit of de Maistre, who in 1796 had insisted that the French revolution had been God's punishment of an irreligious and undutiful nation, was always latent in the French conservative's temperament, and now it surfaced exactly where it might have been expected: in the clergy and the officer corps. A revered old commander, Marshal Pétain, who had been among those who led triumphant France to honor and victory during the First World War, took charge of the government and the stoical duty of redeeming France by endurance of God's just chastisement. French conservatives, and the army in particular, had in any case been ambivalent toward Hitler. Neopagan though Hitler might be, he cherished "blood and soil," fatherland, family, and work—all ideals that French conservatives believed any honorable person should value. During her punishment France could learn from her punisher. The message was reinforced from most Catholic pulpits. There were priests in the resistance and members of conservative families with the Free French, like de Gaulle himself, but most conservatives during the occupation, whatever attitude they laid claim to later, sided with Pétain. Within France the iron grip of the concept grew almost universal: France had sinned; France must bow before God's chastening rod.

In this atmosphere came the performance of Sartre's first play, a retelling of the story of Agamemnon. There was no need to inform the audience that night that they were about to witness a topical allegory. The French were accustomed to seeing their political problems in classical garb. There was Jean Cocteau's famous *The Trojan War Shall Not Take Place*, a retelling during the pacifist prewar years of *Lysistrata*. A play on a classical theme was a political signal. The audience sat back to be instructed.

As the curtain went up, Orestes, whose father Agamemnon had been murdered by his mother and her lover, was shown returning to his native Argos, where his mother and her lover were on the throne. Young Orestes and his tutor were followed by Zeus in disguise, a majestic figure with the unmistakable beard of God the Father, Zeus Ahenobarbos, the famous statue at Palermo. Zeus trapped a black-clad old woman and explained to Orestes that the entire nation of Argos was in mourning because of its remorse for the murder of its rightful king. The old woman, wriggling to escape, assured Zeus, "Oh, sir, I do repent, most heartily I repent. If you only knew how I repent. . . ." Even her little grandson has been brought up in a spirit of repentance. "Though he's only seven, he never plays or laughs, for thinking of his original sin."[6] The stage then showed the Argive ceremony of repentance. In this ceremony a cave was opened once a year and the dead were said by a priest to come forth. The town swarmed with a plague of flies, said by the priests to have been sent by Zeus as carriers of repentance.

A religion of repentance sponsored by a vengeful god —few in defeated and occupied France in 1943 would fail to see a reflection of the myth propagated by the Pétain government: that France had sinned and was being justly punished. *The Flies* was only minutes old before Sartre's audience edged forward in its seats.

Orestes entered repentant Argos as unknowing and uncommitted. Taken away as an infant he had been brought up by some rich Athenians. He was wonderfully free but he lamented the quality of his freedom. There was nothing he could call "mine," neither his adopted Athens nor his native Argos. He had no "purpose." He was "light" and he walked "on air."[7] Sartre described not only the condition of alienated man in general but of French youth in particular, many of whom had seen no more actual fighting in the war than Sartre had, and like him had come home as morally adrift as Orestes returning to Argos, or the young man who came to Sartre for advice about joining the Free French.

The rest of Sartre's play can be regarded as a development of that advice. *The Flies* was a message play, and the message at the minimum created for that audience of 1943 a parallel between the illegitimate tyrants of Argos and the German occupying forces. For those who chose to interpret the message more specifically, the government of France, Pétain's government, was in effect "married" to the German invaders. Clytemnestra, Queen of Argos, and her lover Aegistheus represented the unholy alliance that wed French collaborationists to the enemy.

In this situation Orestes was shown choosing what to do. He determined to kill Clytemnestra and Aegistheus, not in revenge for the murder of his father, but to free the people of Argos from the tyranny backed by the religion of repentance. Aegistheus, Clytemnestra's lover and murderer of Agamemnon, had set up a rule of mystery, miracle, and authority, but Sartre drew him as a new and different type of Grand Inquisitor, one who knew his doom and was weary of the burden of being the only one who understood that human beings were by nature free. Zeus was depicted as the god who had created people free, a force with power over nature but without power over people except the power people give him by belief. Zeus was shown saying, "In the fullness of time a man was to come, to announce my decline."[8] On the stage Orestes was that man. In actuality it was, of course, Jean-Paul Sartre.

Thus Sartre's message in *The Flies* went further than his advice to the young man troubled about his mother, to whom he said in effect, "Make up your own mind." Sartre's message in *The Flies* was quite simply and starkly, "Go out and kill the nearest Nazi; free the people of France." Alerted by the enthusiasm of the audience, the German censors took a closer look at the play and closed it down.

Sartre's vision can thus be seen to contain paradoxes, as if it were somehow the nature of his thought to twist against itself. One must not give advice and so take away freedom, and yet in *The Flies* Sartre gave advice so emotionally compelling that he took away freedom in the very cause of freedom. The twisting, the tension between opposites, a tension that refuses to resolve, so that two contradictory ideas must be held at once was characteristic of Sartre's thought from the beginning. It is in fact the Sartrean consistency. And it is his consistency in this respect that is one of the most important aspects of his vision. It was Sartre's writing, and more than Sartre's writing, Sartre's life, which illustrated the fact that a central change in twentieth-century thinking was a diminution of the concept basic to the Western tradition since Aristotle: that opposites were mutually exclusive in the mind.

Sartre was not the first in the writing of prophetic fiction to show this change. In Switzerland, after the First World War, another writer, who shared Sartre's respect for Dostoevsky, had written of the necessary union of opposites in thought and in life. Hermann Hesse in his enormously popular novel *Siddhartha* had shown his hero arriving at a frame of mind which Siddhartha knew even his best friend Govinda must "think is jest or folly: that is, in every truth the opposite is equally true. For example, a truth can only be expressed and enveloped in words if it is one-sided. Everything that is thought and expressed in words is one-sided, only half the truth; it lacks totality, completeness."[9] For Hesse contradictions coexisted; even opposites were by the very nature of life and thought in simultaneity. Never is a human being "wholly saint or sinner." Even the line "between suffering and bliss, between good and evil, is also an illusion."[10] There could have been no greater contradiction to the whole linear cast of Western thought since the Greeks than Hesse's view, yet the publication in 1922 of *Siddhartha* had taken the youth of defeated Germany by storm, as Sartre's thinking took France by storm in 1943. A freshly defeated people is in process of reassessment, and so is more receptive to innovative states of mind.

It took some time for Sartre's public to understand how deeply he had abandoned traditional linear structures. For an extended period after 1943 it was possible to claim that if one thought contradicted another in Sartre's existentialism, it was because one thought had succeeded another in his ongoing process of existential self-definition. But to claim linearity and noncontradiction for Sartre's thought was difficult even in 1943. And by the nineteen-seventies, when Robert Ornstein and others would point out the value of states of consciousness dependent upon simultaneity rather than succession, the simultaneity of opposites had already made itself known in the Western world through what actually had taken place in the changing texture of thought from the mid-nineteenth century to the mid-twentieth. Often, as with Hesse, the rise of the union of opposites in creative thought was regarded as brought about by infiltration into the logical-linear thinking of Europe of Indian, Chinese, and other Eastern influences. But Sartre apparently developed the intellectual habit of simultaneity of opposites quite spontaneously.

For example, it was perfectly clear that even the Sartre who refused to tell the young man what to do about his mother was in a logical inconsistency. The young man wanted Sartre to tell him what to do. Sartre wanted the young man to make up his own mind what to do. What resulted was a most insistent imposition of the will of Jean-Paul Sartre on the will of the young man, at the same time as the young man remained—at Sartre's insistence—absolutely free.

This sort of paradox was the very texture of Sartre's thought. It is instructive to consider the early Sartre, because in 1943, when Sartre was only thirty-eight, the holding of simultaneous opposites in his mind was still rather elementary compared to his later thinking. And yet, from first to last, simultaneity itself was the same basic paradoxical pattern—all the way from *Being and Nothingness* to *The Critique of Dialectical Reason*.

Several variations on the pattern appear in *The Flies*. Inherent in *Being and Nothingness* was the proposition that although man advanced from past into future by selecting at each instant from alternative courses of action and shaping his essence as he went along, there was one choice he could not make and that was to make no choice at all. Even to refrain from choice was itself a choice. Thus man was "condemned to be free"—the phrase which became Sartre's best known and most accepted paradox. Man was free, and he was not free to be unfree; thus freedom and unfreedom existed simultaneously.

Orestes illustrated both this contradictory kind of freedom and another kind, not contradictory and less defined. The young Orestes, disguised in Argos, gave his name as Philebus, "lover of youth." Sartre took the name from the title of a Platonic dialogue in which Socrates led a disciple to truth. Sartre's Philebus was too "light." He was uncommitted. He had this type of freedom because he had entered into no adequate human relationships. But he was capable of relationship because, unlike his sister Electra, he lived in existential good faith in the present, in the "nothingness" of that balancing point between past and future in which one made up one's mind. Electra, on the other hand, had grown up in Argos dreaming of the day when her brother would arrive. She lived not in the present but in the future, taking her identity from the dream in which she would be one of her father's avengers. She could not enter into true and lasting relationship with her brother because he did not correspond to her dream. She had not dreamed of a free man but of an avenger "tangled up in his destiny, like a horse whose belly is ripped open and his legs are caught up in his guts. . . . So go away, my noble-souled brother. I have no use for noble souls; what I need is an accomplice."[11] Electra was from the beginning the slave of her dream.

Philebus, on the other hand, may be said to have been portrayed as "unconditionally free" at the play's opening, in that it was a freedom without paradox, almost without conscious thought. Philebus was simply an uncommitted youth who lived in the present, not in a dream. But he was as alienated as Electra because he had no commitment.

Without true commitment there was no matrix within which he could relate to his sister, to the people of Argos, or to anyone else. As soon, however, as he committed himself to freeing the people, his "purpose" created meaningful relationships all around him. To the people of Argos, Orestes related as their liberator; to Electra, he related as her "accomplice." He related to the deed he was about to perform and conferred meaning on it. It was not murder; it was liberation.

Sartre intended to show Orestes as an existential hero; Electra, as an existential antiheroine. The difference was to lie in their freedom. One may question, however, if there was as much distinction between them as one might suppose.

Electra, who had focused her whole life on a central event to take place in the future, was incapable of life in the present. As soon as Orestes had killed Aegistheus and Clytemnestra, she began to live in the past, in her memory of their deaths. She committed two existential sins: she lived in the past and she allowed custom and morality to name the deed, which for her then became not liberation but murder. Unable once to relate to her brother because he did not fit her dream of the future avenger, she could not relate to him after the murder because she took her identity, accomplice-to-murder, from the past and the religion of remorse, and would not move on with him into the future and emerge into new being as liberator.

Electra, thus, was not free, nor could she enter into relationship with anyone who was free because no free person could fit into the arbitrary and static vision of the past in which she existed.

But the freedom of Orestes, while it contrasted with Electra's enslavement to the past, was a peculiar and self-contradictory state quite unlike the easy spontaneous freedom he had enjoyed as Philebus. To some degree Sartre warned his audience of this fact. He showed Electra as more terrified of Orestes after the murder than she was of the furies of remorse into which the flies had been transformed. "Those hell-hounds frighten me, but you frighten me still more."[12] She preferred the anguish of repentance for crime rather than a share in the life of Orestes. The preference was not surprising. The freedom of the committed person was, as Sartre showed, a hard path. Aware that he was condemned to be free, a committed person like Orestes must advance steadily into the unknown, shaping his essence by his choices, with no standards to guide him except freedom itself. All choices existed in the condition which Orestes had entered, except the choice not to choose. For the committed man, therefore, freedom and unfreedom coexisted. And for Sartre this unfreedom-in-freedom was the ground of being, out of which each authentic, Orestes-type person surged up to create himself and his destiny.

In any discussion of Sartre and his concept of freedom one must constantly keep in mind its nature both as highest value and as psychological imperative. Although one uses simply the word "freedom," one must not forget that this freedom is paradoxically coercive. One cannot, according to Sartre, not be free once one has ceased to be a Philebus and become an Orestes.

Since freedom in this sense was the ultimate good to which one should bring as many people as possible, and

since this freedom was also the creator of each ongoing authentic personality, one may see that for Sartre this freedom became an ultimate value, man's source and man's
goal, corresponding to the force that in other periods and
cultures was called god or the gods. Between 1930 and
1943, when Sartre was shaping the work eventually to be
published as *Being and Nothingness*, the reconciliation between his concept of freedom and his concept of human
relationships gave him at least as much trouble as any
theologian ever had reconciling a concept of God with a
concept of how human beings are related to it and to one
another. For Sartre every authentic personality was in an
ongoing flux in which he created himself, his own morality,
his own actions, and his own identity. He was thus constantly at odds with others, who were also creating their
own moralities and their own identities. Not only was such
a person at odds with all persons living existentially; he
was also at odds with all those many persons who did not
create their own moralities or identities. These people Sartre called "inauthentic" because, like Electra, they took a
morality from the world around them or an identity from
the remembered past or a dreamed of future—what Sartre
called "bad faith," which was also a choice. As Orestes
tried to persuade Electra to live his way not hers, so every
person was constantly trying to impose his own identity or
morality on those around him. It was indeed the effort in
which Sartre himself, as teacher and anti-Nazi, was most
deeply engaged. No matter that Orestes' course was the
right one and Electra's, the wrong one, that Sartre's es-
pousal of the resistance was "good" (as an instrument of

freedom) against the efforts of the collaborators (as agents of tyranny), the fact remained that his influence impaired the freedom of others to choose for themselves. Like almost everyone else, Sartre thought he knew better than those around him. It was a condition endemic in the modern world whose established moralities had fragmented. All people were in collision with all other people. For each person in the existential flux, the aimed for situation was one in which he could render all others subordinate to his will so that he alone was autonomous. "Man is the being whose project is to be God" Sartre had written in *Being and Nothingness*.[13] Hitler was a man whose project enjoyed exemplary success. Few could equal it, but, according to Sartre, all were making the effort.

Of the many twists that Sartre's thought made against itself, this was the most conspicuous. Sartre loathed the totalitarian solution adopted by Hitler and imposed on France. This loathing shaped all Sartre's subsequent thinking. Let each person, as Sartre taught in *The Flies*, assert his individual freedom, commit that freedom to freedom for all people, and exalt freedom as the one great value. Yet what could be done when these many individuals, these many freedoms, came into collision? How to avoid the frightful "plan to be God"? Sartre saw this problem as the modern world's dilemma. His effort to solve it was to lead him ever deeper into paradox, deeper into the kind of thinking to which we have given the name, simultaneity of opposites.

CHAPTER V

Existentialism, Violence, and Communism

One resolution of the state of atomized warfare in which each person as a self-orienting particularity shaped his own morality and was set against every other person, on whom he tried to impose that morality, was the common adoption of a united and overarching morality to which all could freely subscribe. Sartre came to see international communism as such a morality.

There are many aspects under which one can view Sartre's attraction to marxism. The first is obviously that such an attraction was simply one more of the contradictions Sartre's mind characteristically seemed to generate. His increasing allegiance to a totalitarian philosophy that permitted no individual deviation and at the same time his insistence on individual freedom was finally to form for Sartre the most complex of all his paradoxes. The climax came in 1960 with the publication of *The Critique of Dialectical Reason*. This work, which placed existentialism as an "ideology" *inside* marxism as "the one philosophy" that gave "expression to the general movement of society," was the apotheosis of that tendency in Sartre's thought to set irreconcilable opposites against one another and insist that they can and must be held at the same time.

Violence was a natural concomitant of the early stages of the condition of mind in which opposites were to be held in simultaneity. At the very least the mind, accustomed to linear thinking and unreconciled to the simultaneous existence of opposites within consciousness, did violence to itself. On a larger scale recognition of opposites as coexistent in the outer world caused efforts to suppress one of the opposites and restore the more comfortable unity to which human beings in the West were accustomed. To most "reasonable" people, if class interests were indeed in opposition, there must result a war of class against class; if national interests were in opposition, there must result a war of nation against nation. Sartre, as an early practitioner of the simultaneity of opposites within his own mind, was fascinated by violence of all kinds: the violence of war, the violence of the class struggle, and particularly the psychic violence that, from the time of *Being and Nothingness* in 1943, he saw as an inevitable part of "being with others." Sartre developed a habit of incarnating irreconcilable opposites in his characters, setting them against each other, and then examining the result. Intense inner violence and cruel and thought-provoking reflection on the modern human condition became characteristic of his work.

For example, in his play of 1944, *No Exit*, Sartre presented a study of a personality which engaged in acts of psychic violence upon surrounding personalities. The subject he chose for his drama was a woman, subordinated by her birth as a female—a subordination against which she revolted by becoming a lesbian—and also subordinated by her society, which could find no more meaningful occupation for her than a job as a post-office clerk. Inez, the most vital of the three characters in *No Exit*, had spent her life in the humiliating nothingness of stamping other people's letters. As clerk and woman-rebelling-against-herself so that her very sex was indeterminate, Inez had become a walking zero.

Most of us will recognize Inez. The zero personality has always abounded in what Dostoevsky called the ant heap. Sartre saw such personalities as plunged into deepest anguish, for they were living creatures being forced toward nothingness. Treated as objects by others, they could not even be sure they existed.

Sartre set his play in a mythical "hell." Life has ended, there are no more ongoing choices, and three people must face what they are. Garcin is a coward who died betraying his revolutionary comrades. Estelle is a young woman who murdered her baby. They have never known each other during life but are to be confined with Inez for all eternity.

There are no self-reflecting mirrors in hell, and Estelle asks Inez if her lipstick is smudged. Inez tells her that it is, and Estelle quickly repairs the damage, saying with a glance at Garcin, "Luckily no one has seen me."[1] Inez is "no one" in Estelle's consciousness. But in Inez's own con-

sciousness she is not "no one" but "someone," an autonomous being who is in love with Estelle. Two persons are
simultaneously holding contradictory concepts about the
identity of one of them. According to Sartre's thinking at
this time, such a situation gives rise to violent collision.
How does a "no one" emerge from the condition of being a zero to someone else? If I am Inez seated next to you,
and you, like Estelle, ignore my existence, there is one way
in which I can force you to acknowledge that I do exist.
I can pinch you until you say "ouch." I am then certain I
have existence for you because you have just assured me of
it. Magnify the "ouch" situation a thousand times and there
results the torturer or the murderer, for whom the world
must constantly provide victims in order that the torturing
or the murderous personality can keep from sliding back
into the zero from which it has emerged. Inez is both torturer and murderer; she has spent her life being both.

As Sartre saw it, violence is always latent in and around
the Inez's of this world. The accuracy of the vision seems
indisputable. The violence of the criminal, the sadist, or
simply the tormenting member of a family who must constantly reassure himself or herself of existence and significance by causing suffering to others, are known to most of
us. Sartre's diagnosis, however, was far more penetrating
than anybody's day-to-day observation of the average zero
personality in the average ant heap.

A zero personality can exercise its violence upon any
living creature which is capable of pain and which comes
over the horizon. However, certain personalities, which also
abound in the ant heap, are particularly vulnerable. These

are carefully sought-out victims because their suffering is
specially delectable for their torturers. Estelle and Garcin
are such personalities. Garcin has lived his life convincing
others that he is a "tough guy."[2] Estelle, the killer of her
illegitimate child, has lived pretending to be an innocent
and attractive ingenue, to her admirers a "crystal girl, a
glancing stream."[3] Thus both are what Sartre calls "inauthentic," taking from outside themselves identities that in
inward actuality they do not have. Both want to continue
the process. Estelle is eager to assure Garcin that he is a
brave man, if he will in return assure her that she is an attractive woman.[4] Unfortunately for them, however, Inez is
there to delight in asserting her own existence by telling
them both the truth. "What a lovely scene: coward Garcin
holding baby-killer Estelle in his manly arms!"[5] Sartre's
implication was that an Inez is always "there." There is
always someone viewing us who can do violence to the images of ourselves we have created, and there is no greater
torture. "Hell is—other people!"[6] The violence of Sartre's
hell propagates violent retaliation. Estelle stabs Inez. Symbolically Inez cannot die. For one thing, an inhabitant of
hell is already dead. For another, Inez is "a gaze observ-
ing you, a formless thought that thinks you"[7] and as such
she exists in the mind as long as the mind remembers her,
whether she is dead or not.

The interesting thing about *No Exit* was, however, less
in its disclosure of psychological relationships between people than of relationships within the mind, particularly
within Sartre's own thought. As Garcin and Estelle were
dependent on their torturer Inez, who destroyed their iden-

tities as fast as they could build them up, so there seems to have been in Sartre's thought a force that surged up from the freedom of his mind and tried to attack all contradictory coexisting conclusions as quickly as he formulated them. Sartre examined a type of violence in *No Exit* that seems to have existed within himself.

For instance, in 1948 Sartre, seconded by a somewhat reluctant Albert Camus, who was becoming apolitical at the same time as Sartre was becoming increasingly politicized, founded a French marxist party intended to provide Frenchmen of the left with an alternative to the traditional French communism directed from Moscow. In that year Sartre brought out a new play, *Dirty Hands*, whose existentialist hero was a communist schismatic. Schism from the party line reflected Sartre's and Camus's own Rassemblement Démocratique Révolutionnaire. Sartre portrayed his hero, Hoederer, as an existentially authentic man who adopted marxist policy to the ongoing nature of reality, which Hoederer saw as superseding orders handed down at a distance in space and time by a central bureaucracy in the Soviet Union. Hoederer believed that people were more important than principles[8] and to save "hundreds of thousands" of lives at the end of the war[9] was willing not only to go against the Soviet Communist party line but was willing to form an alliance with the bourgeois and monarchist parties.

Dirty Hands was an effective play and a popular one—too popular. In 1954, when he attended an international peace conference in Vienna where *Dirty Hands* was in rehearsal, Sartre at a press conference objected to its being produced—ostensibly because the play would strengthen tension between East and West.[10] But the real reasons were probably different. By 1954 Sartre's own communist party had died for lack of funds. Also, *Dirty Hands* had been greeted by European anticommunists as showing the divisions within communism as well as communism's innate brutality. (Sartre dramatized Hoederer's assassination as ordered by his own party.) A third reason, though, for Sartre's objection to the Vienna performance was perhaps more important. Hoederer had been portrayed as basically a man of peace and compromise. But in 1954 Sartre was going through a stage of no longer believing in compromise. The death of his own revolutionary party had created too great a trauma. He had come to believe that only violent revolution of the Russian type was possible in the modern world.

In 1951, three years after *Dirty Hands*, Sartre had brought out a play about a leader of the Peasants' Revolt in Germany, a movement that Engels had seen as a forerunner of the proletarian revolution of the future. Sartre's hero, Goetz, was a metaphysical rebel.[11] Goetz was a man who believed in God but also fanatically sought his own identity. He attempted first to establish freedom by becoming an evildoer, a monster of crime and massacre, God's opposite. This identity crumbled when he discovered that his actual wish was to do good and that millions of evildoers existed in the world while sanctity was so infrequent as to be nearly unique. Goetz then founded the "City of the Sun," an artificial kingdom of peace and happiness in the midst of the misery and slaughter in Germany. Inevitably the pacifist City of the Sun was sacked and overrun. Goetz achieved his identity in the end only when he realized that God did not exist and that man must shape his own fate by uniting in violent insurrection with the peasants against the landowners. Where Hoederer, the man of compromise and humanity, had wished to save "hundreds of thousands of lives" by working from within an alliance of opposites, Goetz at the close of *The Devil and the Good Lord* stabbed a peasant soldier on his own side for disobedience and declared that from now on he would be "a hangman and a butcher."[12] It was as if the psychic violence chronic in Sartre's work from the beginning had during this period been externalized. In the violent world, no City of the Sun could survive. Since the world lived by the sword, all must take to the sword.

If Sartre's thought turned once more upon itself between *Dirty Hands* in 1948 and *The Devil and the Good Lord* in 1951, circumstances soon afterwards caused another reversal, particularly ironic just at the time when Sartre had espoused violence as a necessary political instrument. Since 1946, Russia had been viewed by many Europeans as a guardian of peace, while America, especially during the period of John Foster Dulles's "brinkmanship," had seemed to Europeans to carry the forces of war. Then in 1956 the image of the Soviet Union was drastically altered. Russia brutally crushed the Hungarian revolt. Men, women, and young people joined hands and opposed their bodies to Soviet tanks in the streets of Budapest. Sartre, the apostle of violence in theory, experienced revulsion at this demonstration of the nature of violence in fact. In 1950 he had justified North Korean aggression by violence and had alienated Camus by seeming to condone the Russian concentration camps. In 1954, after a trip to Russia, he had declared that he found in this country of Solzhenitsyn a "complete freedom of criticism."[13] But the crushing of the Hungarian revolt was an open declaration of the right of violence to destroy Sartre's most cherished value: self-determination. One may ask how much self-determination Goetz at the end of *The Devil and the Good Lord* left the peasant soldier he killed. But the only consistency Sartre's thought ever had was its inconsistency. Once more he rounded upon his earlier self. Invited by a Polish review to discuss "the situation of existentialism in 1957," he began the work that eventually resulted in the enormous *Critique of Dialectical Reason*, a fascinating disclosure of the development of his type of consciousness.

Sartre stated first of all that marxism was unsurpassable as the philosophy of "our time"[14] and was the one all-inclusive vital force from which the human race must take its nature and its future. So far, any marxist reader was in agreement. The problem came with what Sartre wanted this all-inclusive force to include. He wanted it to include existentialist freedom as inserted within the classical marxist dogma of the historical determinism of mass societies.[15] Freedom and determinism, the atomized particularity of the individual and the solidarity of the mass—those two traditional opposites, individualism and solidarity—were to coexist, and not only in Sartre's thought, which for decades had on occasion been able to maintain incompatible opposites in simultaneous existence, but in the world of praxis, where Sartre had usually regarded the simultaneous existence of opposites as an inevitable precondition of psychic violence as in *No Exit*, or of actual violence as in *The Devil and the Good Lord.* The placing of existentialism as an "ideology" within dialectical materialism the "philosophy" was not as modest as it appeared. Sartre's theory gave the ideology of existentialism a vital and directive role within the philosophy of marxism, rather as if a big ship had taken on a small but determined pilot, whose resolve was to alter the course established by the ship's officers. One recalls Sartre's observation in *Being and Nothingness* that every person's project is the plan to be God. From this time on, international communism of the Soviet variety lost whatever tolerance it had ever had for Sartre. He was grouped among the pernicious "bourgeois philosophers," whose work was to be swept away by the revolution they impeded.

This rejection made little difference to Sartre. He believed that in any case communism had ceased temporarily its dialectical advance and had become petrified into stasis by ruling bureaucracies that took their character from past events and past ideas. By the very nature of stasis the bureaucracies thus did violence to reality, whose essential characteristic was ongoing motion. Unable to acknowledge errors, the bureaucracies were contradicted at every moment by the rush of events: "the planification imposed by a bureaucracy that would not recognize its errors became by this fact itself a violence against reality."[16]

Sartre thus accused the communist systems of his time of committing the greatest existentialist sin, of being in stasis and taking identity from the past. It would seem, however, that the moment any system of communism would cease to be thus in stasis, would abandon its rigid structure, and would commence to exist as an ongoing flux, there would begin again the conflict of all against all which had been the moral condition of Sartre's existentialism in 1943, and which had appeared to be solved, or at least mitigated, by his adoption of communism as an overarching morality to which all were to subscribe. In Sartre's vision of what marxism should become by incorporating freedom, the coherence that had been marxism's chief gift to Sartre would always be in danger of slipping back into the chaos that had made marxism necessary for Sartre in the first place—and, as he saw it, necessary for the world. Yet to Sartre himself this may not have seemed a serious problem. It was, Sartre believed, man's nature to be a creature between being and nothingness. While marxists regarded Sartre as taking away from them what they most valued, their monolithic consistency, Sartre would see himself simply as restoring marxism to the reality of being as it actually was. And in a period in which the monolithic character that once stamped marxism was obviously proving untenable—as China confronted Russia, as rebel thinkers within the Soviet Union attracted worldwide attention, as contending factions writhed against each other inside the Chinese straitjacket, Sartre's *Critique* seemed more and more cogent.

The aspect of the *Critique* most typical of Sartre came, however, when he got to the heart of the matter and wanted to establish a viable interplay between human beings as separated self-determining particles and human beings as determined by their class and their time in history, taking their being not from freedom, existentialism's supreme value, but from the dialectical struggle between historical forces, the supreme value of dialectical materialism. What developed in Sartre's thought now was no less than a conflict between opposing gods of the post-Christian ideological religions: marxism, which saw historical determinism as man's creator, and existentialism, which saw freedom as the source of man's self-creation. Sartre's resolution was of course paradox. He insisted that there was no struggle. The individualism of the existential credo and the solidarity of the marxist, although opposites, could and must exist in coherent simultaneity.

His solution, characteristic though it was, has probably been more difficult than any other aspect of his recent thought for the habitually linear mind to assimilate. It is, therefore, not surprising that it has attracted less attention than his earlier theories. When it did attract attention, it often met brusque dismissal. Yet his ideas were carefully thought through, and it is possible to find them convincing. For example, while Sartre acknowledged that the great individuals of history—men like Napoleon, for instance— were products of historical forces which if they had not produced a Napoleon would have produced someone like him, Sartre insisted as well that human beings, although shaped by history, also shaped the history that shaped them. Furthermore, they created the characters and opportunities of the human beings who were to come after them. Sartre made this claim not only for Napoleons but for countless ordinary people whose lives seemed outwardly inconsequential but whose actions were of great significance.

The illustration he gave was an episode of a young black, part of a ground crew at an airport near London, who seized an aircraft and, although he had never piloted a plane, flew it across the Channel. It was unthinkable in that time and place that a black man should fly, should act as pilot. This interdiction was for him a subjective privation, but with his act of defiance subjectivity passed into the objective world. The "*general* revolt" of the colored races against their exploiters, whether colonial or international, expressed itself "*in him,*" a particular individual. Thus, particular individuals, especially when they undertook a novel and extreme action in tune with the historical current of their time, shaped the historical current which was also shaping them and added to the force that would go on to shape others. The young black in question was all the more "*individual*" and "unique" because his country habitually gave publicity to acts of individualism, and his influence was magnified accordingly.[17]

There was a relationship between this political vision of Sartre's and Dostoevsky's earlier vision of a living sea of human beings who passed from one to another the vibrations of their acts. Dostoevsky had believed that the theological vision which he saw as the thematic climax of *The Brothers Karamazov* was incompatible with political visions of any sort, particularly with the vision of Ivan. Yet obviously Sartre developed a political vision that much resembled the theological vision of Dostoevsky. The resemblance was due, I believe, not to any influence in this regard of Dostoevsky on Sartre, but to the fact that Sartre observed in the Europe of his day a later development of the same mass situation that Dostoevsky had observed in the Russia of his own time. In increasingly bureaucratized societies there was a growth both in alienation, particularly in its form as individual and independent self-assertion,[18] and in its counterforce: the solidarity that developed to answer alienation by creating meaningful human interaction between people who in the shrinking world were necessarily in closer and closer contact.

The most interesting aspect of Sartre's vision in *The Critique of Dialectical Reason* was the recurrence of the coexistence of opposites. Sartre would not surrender historical determinism. What he said of his ideology of particular acts was: "As long as one has not studied the structures of the future in a determined society, one necessarily exposes oneself to understanding nothing about social forces."[19] What he meant by "structures" was set forth in his anecdote of the young black. If Sartre would not give up social determinism, neither would he give up personal self-determination. Only the simultaneous existence, and the interpenetration in which each shaped the other, corresponded to what he believed he saw in the reality of his era.

What Sartre was describing was a vision of the human condition according to which each person was able to retain the power of personal self-determination while also acting in concert with all other persons similarly endowed. Sartre thus became another thinker who made a resolute attack upon the modern world's most violent problem: the seeming impossibility of reconciling individual freedom with mass solidarity. Dostoevsky had seen the solution in terms of mutually exclusive opposites. Sartre saw opposites as capable of existing together and developing together. People with linear consciousness must perhaps accuse Sartre of contradiction. But, as we have seen, contradiction had always been the essence of Sartre's thought at its most significant and most vital.

CHAPTER VI

Albert Camus
and the World of the Absurd

If Sartre's vision was above all political and he was, like Ivan Karamazov, a visionary whose focus was primarily on political change, the vision of Albert Camus renounced political solutions. According to Camus, all revolutionaries imposed reigns of terror and created tyrannies more absolute than those they overthrew. Since 1789 man's area of freedom had been narrowing, not enlarging. The modern world was, Camus believed, on the path to the greatest tyrannies of all time. In *The Rebel* in 1951, the mature Camus (he was thirty-eight, the same age as Sartre when in 1943 he had dramatized his views in *The Flies*) saw both the nineteenth-century thought of Ivan Karamazov and the twentieth century's practice of marxism as inimical to all immediate hope for the exercise of humanity's right to happiness.

The difference between the early lives of Sartre and Camus is significant. Sartre's biographical treatment of Genet and Flaubert portrayed each as the product of a particular childhood. Sartre's own autobiography, *The Words*, gave its entire two hundred and fifty-five pages to describing his life to the age of eleven. Sartre in his grandfather's household was a prototype of his future. "Be careful," his much put-upon young widowed mother used to whisper to the coddled and brilliant boy of whom so much was expected, "we're not in our own home."[1]

Young Jean-Paul thus existed as an alien and particularized splinter inserted into the mass of the respected Professor Charles Schweitzer's family. It was in miniature the same stubborn individualism, verging upon impertinence, with which Sartre later inserted existentialism as an autonomous splinter into the massive body of world communism.

The young Sartre was both determining and self-determined. Like the youthful revolutionary intellectual, Hugo, in Sartre's play *Dirty Hands* (1948), Sartre learned in childhood to despise the privileges, the arrogance, the exploitiveness, and the hypocrisy of the bourgeoisie into which he had been born. Every member of the Schweitzer family, except Jean-Paul's mother, the gentle Anne-Marie, was poised against every other in the violent mutual antagonism which divided that peculiar household. Hatred is not too strong a word to use to express the emotion with which Sartre regarded this background. Nevertheless, this background made him what he later became.

If hatred was Sartre's reaction to his childhood, the reaction of Camus to his own family was totally different—

love touched by compassion. If it is true that a man who has had compassion on himself is a man who will have compassion on others, the following passage from Camus's recollections may be significant:

> I remember a child who lived in a poor section . . . the staircase was not lighted. Even now, many years later, he could find his way in that house in the dark. . . . His legs remember the exact height of the steps; his hand, its instinctive, never-dominated horror of the bannisters . . . because of the roaches.[2]

Camus's mother was a scrubwoman. She was a widow and deaf but she was the sole support of her two sons, her old mother, and her crippled half brother, all of whom lived together in an Algerian slum. Camus's childhood role in his household was that of explainer and intercessor. He would shout necessary information into the ear of his deaf mother. This was much the same as Camus's later role as playwright, editor, and writer—shouting at the deaf, or nearly deaf, France he loved.

The boy was not unhappy. He had the beautiful beaches of Algiers with their tropical sun and water. At school a perceptive teacher discovered his gifts and got him a scholarship to the Lycée d'Alger. Then at seventeen Camus was diagnosed as tubercular. Just as life was brightening, he received the sentence of death which during his most formative years he expected to be carried out at any time.

He worked his way through the university by taking menial and clerical jobs. At twenty-one he joined the Communist party. He left, ostensibly because of resentment at the party's indifference to the plight of the Algerian Arabs, but his actual reasons probably also had much to do with his traumatized sensitivity to death. In *The Plague*, Tarrou, whose physical description Camus made resemble his own, explained that he became a rebel against the government because the government killed, and a rebel against revolution because revolutionaries also killed. An alienated wanderer, he decided to "leave it to others to make history."[3]

For the generation of postwar alienated European and American youth,[4] Camus's novel, *The Stranger*,[5] published in 1942, expressed the nature of the alienated personality in a death-dealing, unjust, and absurd world. It is a mistake to suppose that Meursault (the name suggested "death-jump") directly represented Camus himself in his youth. The first conspicuous signal Camus's novel gave of the psychological condition of Meursault was that Meursault did not cry at his mother's funeral. Camus, on the contrary, deeply loved and responded to his mother. Meursault was not so much Camus as a type Camus observed in the Algiers of the late nineteen-thirties. The type may have been latent in Camus, although it was not as actualized as in Meursault. And in time Camus would leave completely behind whatever aspects of character he did share with Meursault. He did no doubt share some. *The Myth of Sisyphus*, worked out in the same period as *The Stranger*, indicated that to a certain degree Camus himself was involved in this alienated frame of mind.

Meursault existed as if enclosed in glass. He neither gave nor received emotion. Nor did any concepts—for example, of morality—reach Meursault. When a "friend," Raymond, asked Meursault to join him in a scheme to beat the friend's Arab mistress, Meursault agreed. Meursault did not consent out of loyalty and affection for his "friend," because Meursault, the "stranger," experienced loyalty and affection for no one. He simply did not see any reason why he should not oblige Raymond "as I'd no cause not to satisfy him." Unlike Camus, who had an impassioned and indignant pity for the Moors of Algeria, Meursault felt no pity for the Arab girl. Empathy was entirely unknown to him. In an essay written during these years, Camus revealed that for the omnipresent creature he called "the absurd man," Ivan Karamazov's "everything is permitted" was simply a condition of a universe in which there was no meaning. While the absurd did not "authorize all actions," it did in praxis confer "an equivalence on the consequences of those actions."[6]

Meursault was the absurd man depicted in extreme form. For him all aspects of life were equivalent. His mother's death, his sleeping with his girl the following night, his boss's offer of a promotion, all these were of equal value in his consciousness—all left him equally apart and insulated. How a person became a Meursault was depicted in another early essay. "Rising, streetcar, four hours in the office or factory, meal, streetcar, four hours of work, meal, sleep, and Monday Tuesday Wednesday Thursday Friday and Saturday according to the same rhythm."[7] To Camus such a life resembled that of Sisyphus, compelled in Hades forever to roll a rock to the top of a mountain only to see it roll down again. Why not commit suicide? The reason for holding on to life was what Camus called "lucidity": Sisyphus developed clear recognition of his condition. With recognition came a certain type of satisfaction. "At each of those moments when he leaves the heights and gradually sinks toward the lairs of the gods, he is superior to his fate. He is stronger than his rock."[8] Camus wrote, "There is no fate that cannot be surmounted by scorn." He concluded the essay by saying, "One must imagine Sisyphus happy."[9]

In *The Stranger*, after the Arab girl was beaten by Raymond, some Arabs bent on harassment and possibly revenge, followed Raymond, Meursault, and Meursault's girl to a beach, where Meursault, like the young Camus, often went to enjoy the sun and water. Meursault, who had Raymond's gun with him, was wandering the beach when he came upon one of the Arabs. A knife glinted in the Arab's hand. The sun was hot on Meursault's head and dazzling on the knife. By reflex Meursault fired. The shot killed the Arab. "I knew I'd shattered the balance of the day, the spacious calm of this beach on which I had been happy. But I fired four more shots into the inert body."[10] The first shot was neither willed nor unwilled. The undifferentiated consciousness of Meursault simply exploded into violence without realization. The four added shots expressed his rage at this act which, after it was performed, he recognized as his "undoing." The way in which violence was a part of undifferentiation and how it inevitably exploded was sparingly but effectively described by Camus. In a personality like Meursault's, unaccustomed to seeing any reasons for or against any given action, the reflex of violence, the tightening of a finger upon a trigger, met no inhibitions. It was a psychological condition familiar to anyone who had ever lived in a slum, or had known the psychology of ant heap inhabitants of whatever class.

In Part II of the book, Camus, having examined the violence in Meursault, the unrelating, alienated man, examined the violence in the society that had created him. In prison a magistrate shook a crucifix at Meursault and shouted at him to believe in God. But Meursault simply did not believe and said so. At his trial, the jury convicted him unhesitatingly. The accidental aspect of the murder, the obvious element of self-defense, were eclipsed by the prosecution's evocation of the nature of this young man who had not cried at his mother's funeral. The social foundations of a hypocritical world, precariously sustaining or pretending to sustain standards that it had long ago left behind, trembled at the existence of a Meursault.

Meanwhile Meursault proceeded ever further into the lucidity that was for Camus the consolation of the Sisyphus personality. Meursault attacked in outrage the priest who came to urge him to repent. He realized that he had often been happy in the sea and on the beaches. He understood the "benign indifference of the universe," which was so much like his own state of consciousness. He then rose to what was for Camus at that time the culminating state of recognition for a Meursault, which Camus showed as the only possible way that in his circumstances he could relate to the world of humanity, the one road out of solitude for a "stranger." "For all to be accomplished, for me to feel less lonely, all that remained was to hope that on the day of my execution there should be a huge crowd of spectators and that they should greet me with howls of execration."[11]

The greater the rage of the world, the more powerful the challenge to scorn. The cherishing of scorn as the one satisfying mode of relating to a world whose state of meaninglessness made it unjust—not even consciously unjust but unjust out of hypocrisy, the crumbling of social values, and the indifference of the universe—was a reflex much like that of old Fyodor Karamazov. But Meursault was a far more extreme manifestation of alienation in the human ant heap of French Algeria sixty years after Dostoevsky had dramatized similar reactions in late Tsarist Russia.

Camus would leave Meursault behind in his own development, but it seems doubtful that the ordinary person in the period after the Second World War did so quite as successfully. The cities of the Western world swarmed with Meursaults. Those who were in college at any time from 1946 to the 1960s know that in those years at least ten to twenty percent of young first readers of *The Stranger* felt they were meeting aspects of themselves in Camus's Meursault. With *The Stranger*, Camus became Pied Piper to large segments of the youth of the West, leading the way the scorn he mythologized in Sisyphus.

At first Sartre saw Camus as an embryo existentialist and hailed *The Stranger* with excitement and enthusiasm. He was eight years older than Camus and had never had a father; he enjoyed fathering Camus. And, quite obviously, Camus, who had never had a father either, enjoyed being fathered. This relationship continued until both men, whose fathers had abandoned them by death, also abandoned each other. Each became as "dead" to the other as was possible for two such completely exacerbated antagonists. Even when they were no longer speaking, they contradicted one another by their very existence and by the fact that both continued publishing. What kept the breach between them so bitterly unhealed was their different interpretation of a concept central to them both, the nature and the limits of rebellion.

Camus dealt with the problem as early as his play *Caligula* in 1944. In the play he presented the young Roman emperor as a model ruler until the death of his beautiful sister and mistress Drusilla. Then Caligula—either the reigning madman in an empire of the sane, or the one sane person in a world where all the rest preferred to remain mad (the spectator could take either view)—started to teach his people to recognize the truth about the meaningless universe as he himself had been forced to recognize it by the death of Drusilla. Caligula instituted a reign of terror. He tortured and executed subjects, innocent or guilty. It made no difference, since all human beings were condemned to death anyhow. Only the time and the particular agony was to be determined, and this in no logical relationship to innocence or guilt, youth or age. They were condemned as Drusilla had been, by a force utterly indifferent, the "nothing"[12] behind the nature of things, within which all people were compelled to exist from the moment of their birth into the absurd world. Caligula shut the granaries, and so decreed famine—as nature decrees famine—for no reason. Terrible though his efforts were, Caligula lamented that all his executions had been unable to compete with the mortality caused by a single epidemic or one well-waged war.[13]

As saints traditionally "imitated" God, Caligula was a sort of saint of the absurd. He imitated no-god, the "nothing" behind the universe. Thus he was the only human being ever to have truly possessed himself of freedom, a cosmic freedom. The strongest bond that might restrain his freedom and therefore limit his rebellion was love. Caligula had a friend, Scipio, and he had Caesonia, who remained his mistress after the death of Drusilla. He tortured Scipio's father to death, but he left Scipio alive so that Scipio's hatred might attack and destroy their bond of friendship and so free Caligula of his love for his friend. Caesonia, Caligula's mistress, Caligula strangled with his own hands. Caesonia died still loving the monster whose motivations she comprehended. Scipio, too, understood Caligula and did not hate him. In his quest for freedom, therefore, Caligula failed, for he could not free himself of love. He loved Caesonia and he loved Scipio, and they loved him.

Caligula failed equally in his lesson to his people. He started out to teach them the nature of the state of being, the character of the absurd world, by making his own kingdom a microcosm of its horror and injustice. This lesson was, however, only a prelude. The essence of Caligula's teaching was that the state of being was unendurable. All must rebel against it. The people did finally rebel and planned Caligula's assassination. Caligula represented the state of being. He wished his people to comprehend through him the nature of the cosmos and to attack and destroy that nature in the symbolic act of destroying their tyrant, who had embodied the absurd cosmos in himself. Caligula was thus, as Camus called him in the "Preface," "a superior suicide."[14] But what motivated the assassins of Caligula was not anger at the state of being but the emperor's threat to the wealth, pride, ease, and security of their lives. Cherea, the leader of the conspirators, was a wiser and a nobler man, but he too did not rebel against the state of being, but against the condition of knowledge Caligula wanted his people to assimilate. This assimilation was precisely what Cherea refused. Cherea represented those who simply wanted to live, delude themselves, and be happy. Such people were the destroyers of Caligula, not the clearsighted, freed people Caligula had envisioned himself as creating.

Caligula made two summarizing statements at the end of the play. One was, "My freedom isn't the right one."[15] Caligula had described what he was rebelling against as the fact that "men die and they are not happy."[16] He had said, "I want the moon,"[17] and he had set out to make the "impossible possible."[18] Somewhere on the other side of the effort of making the impossible possible, the moon could be grasped, the impossible would become possible, the perfect world kingdom that all tyrants from Napoleon through Hitler had sought as coming into being on the other side of their bloodshed would actually begin to exist. But as the conspirators advanced to kill him, Caligula gave his exclamation that his freedom was the wrong one. The reason behind his cry was that he had discovered that his goal was unattainable. But as he fell before the knives of his assassins, he cried out, "I'm still alive." These were the last words of the play. Camus was saying that in an absurd world the rebellion of Caligulas must occur over and over again. He was also saying that such unlimited rebellion by 1944, when the defeat of Hitler was becoming each day more inevitable, had displayed its true character as being forever doomed.

Only a few years later Camus applied the same reasoning to Soviet communism. He and Sartre were then engaged in their attempt to form an alternate party of the French Marxist Left under Sartre's leadership. A refugee came from Russia with reports of conditions in Soviet labor camps. Camus wanted to publish them. He felt that to inflict such suffering on human beings was beyond the rights of any revolution. It led to tyranny and ultimately to absurdity. Sartre, on the other hand, saw that French Rightists would make political capital out of any revelation of what was happening within the Soviet camps. Sartre believed the information should not be published because he was convinced that the only hope for the freedom of the masses of the world lay with communism. Camus, on the other hand, believed that revolutions only imposed tyrannies more absolute and horrors more terrible than those against which revolutionaries revolted. Sartre and Camus quarreled. After Camus's essay *The Rebel*, published in 1951, defined Camus's belief in the necessity of limits in rebellion and openly attacked marxism, the quarrel became final.

CHAPTER VII

Absurd Reasoning
and the Saints without God

It was curiously characteristic of both Sartre and Camus to show rebellion as based on metaphysical revolt. The first antagonist chosen by Sartre's revolutionary, Goetz, in *The Devil and the Good Lord* was God. One must bear in mind that Sartre developed his view of freedom as that from which each person surged up to create his own essence. What Sartre termed "freedom" more and more took the place of what other persons and other eras had regarded as the value beyond all other values, the goal and the source of human life. As such it eventually assumed the coloring former cultures and former times had given the sacred. It is no exaggeration to say that Sartre came to resemble Dostoevsky's Father Zossima, who longed for a divinized humanity. The revolution of Goetz, like the intellectual revolution of Sartre, displaced the Christian God for a new power that was to shape paradise to come. In emphasizing this aspect of revolution, Sartre may have been reflecting aspects of marxism's classic view of itself as creator of a new Eden. What was altogether new with Sartre, however, was the way in which he incorporated his view of freedom *within* marxism. He envisioned a duality: freedom existing within the world communism whose static bureaucracies, he believed, had betrayed both freedom and the ongoing nature of reality.

A very similar simultaneity of opposites eventually became central also in the entirely different and apolitical thinking of Albert Camus. As early as *The Stranger*, Camus portrayed nature under two opposing aspects. At the funeral of Meursault's mother the sky was a "blaze of light, and the air stoking up rapidly." The "full glare of the morning sun" had "something inhuman" about it.[1] When Meursault killed the Arab, the sun was blazing so fiercely that it seemed "becalmed in a sea of molten steel."[2] On the other hand, when Meursault arrived at the beach with Marie, the sun and the sea were tranquil, luminous, mild. He and Marie lay "basking in sunlight"[3] and, when they swam, the water enfolded them deliciously.

Camus put similar contrast into *Caligula*. Nature was shown as beautiful at the same time as it was terrible. Indeed the beauty was in some sense dependent on the terror. The emperor forced his poets into a contest. The subject assigned was death. The winning poem was Scipio's:

> Pursuit of happiness that purifies the heart,
> Skies rippling with light,
> O wild, sweet, festal joys, frenzy without hope![4]

It was during the scene in which Scipio realized that Caligula comprehended the meaning of his poem that Scipio understood how similar were their views of the cosmos, though Caligula was, as he himself said, "single-minded . . . for evil," while Scipio was "single-minded for good."[5] Neither could endure the contradiction between the beauty of the universe and the cruelty of the universe. Scipio focused on the former, and in his life as a poet dedicated himself to affirmation, truth, and beauty in the sort of lucid rejoicing which did not deny despair.

Camus's greatest novel, *The Plague*, was published in 1947 when Sartre and Camus were at the height of their friendship and saw themselves as allies who had just emerged successfully from the struggle of the French underground against the Nazi tyranny. The occupying brownshirts had been called in France *la peste brune*, so Camus's parable in calling his novel *La Peste, The Plague*, was obvious. It was easy for insiders to see in the humane and efficiently scientific Dr. Rieux, Camus's anti-Nazi philosopher friend Jean-Paul Sartre, while Camus himself appeared as Dr. Rieux's comrade-in-arms, the wandering ex-revolutionary, Tarrou, whose enthusiasm for rugby and whose physical appearance made his reflection of the author most tempting as a surmise, if not a certainty.

The plague that struck the Algerian town of Oran in Camus's novel represented more than the Nazi occupation of France, however. To Camus, evil was beyond politics, war, conquest, or even human psychology. Like flood, fire, and volcanic eruption, evil was a part of nature. At the time Camus wrote *The Plague*, his very title expressed the fact that he saw evil as a disease. Man was an accessory but he was not the cause of evil—at least not the sole cause nor the chief cause.

To be sure, the population of Oran before the plague was not favorably depicted. Camus described the people as a swarm of self-centered atoms, "making money, as much as possible," while in the erotic sphere the "men and women consume one another rapidly in what is called 'the act of love,' or else settle down to a mild habit of conjugality."[6] Even Dr. Rieux had succumbed to this form of nonlife. Seeing his sick wife off to a sanitarium, he could not think what to say to her until she was on the train and he himself was standing outside, with the glass of the train window dividing their separated selves. Camus remarked that the whole town was huddled on its hill, as if deliberately turning its back to the sea, which for Camus was the symbol of vitality.

There was solidarity in the town, however. It was the lifelessly monolithic solidarity of the governing bureaucracy, the solidarity that Camus saw as the concomitant phenomenon of the people's atomized noncommunity. When the rats first began to die in the streets, the government hastened to reassure the people that the phenomenon was meaningless. When the first men and women were stricken and died, the government did not send for serum or impose a quarantine. A few notices were posted to the effect that cases of "fever" had been reported.[7] If the government was careful not to spread the alarming news and chose to post the notices as inconspicuously as possible, the public cooperated by paying no attention. It was the same sort of artificial and lethal solidarity in which the people of France joined their government in slumbering from 1932 to 1938 as Hitler's designs became more and more obvious, and the "plague" that would strike France made its threat more and more clear.

Against the "happy," oblivious city of Oran the plague rose, spread, killed, and receded. It had not been defeated by its victims, of whom thousands died in agony, but withdrew as mysteriously as it had come, as if sinking back temporarily into a vast reservoir of evil. Camus had called Dostoevsky a prophet.[8] Haunted by the ideas Dostoevsky had given to Ivan Karamazov, particularly by Ivan's sensitivity to the suffering of children, Camus made the plague's central and most symbolic victim a child, and the place of the child's agony a converted hospital in what had once been a school. The plague was the stricken child's school of suffering, which also "schooled" the equally helpless Tarrou and Rieux, together with a "learned and militant Jesuit," who in a sermon had told the people of Oran that "this plague came from God for the punishment of their sins" to lead them to repentance.[9] This type of religious blasphemy had been latent in the French religious consciousness since de Maistre, and had been bitterly attacked by Sartre in *The Flies*. At the end of the child's agony, in which his arms and legs were spread out by the glandular swellings as if he were the living X of one more statistic, or as if he were on the cross,[10] Dr. Rieux turned fiercely to the priest: "That child, anyhow, was innocent, and you know it as well as I do!"[11] In his next sermon the priest, Father Paneloux, spoke of the suffering of children, and he no longer emphasized punishment but the mystery of faith in God. "My brothers . . . we must believe everything or deny everything. And who among you, I ask, would dare deny everything?"[12]

Thus Father Paneloux had a change of character. He no longer harangued from his pulpit as if from the height of a moral superiority embodied in organized religion, but instead called all mankind his "brothers" in the unity of tragic ignorance. But Camus, who was keenly anticlerical and shared many of Sartre's views about the role of the Catholic Church in France during the occupation, was not merciful in his final portrait of Father Paneloux. The Jesuit became ill—it might have been plague, it might have been a "doubtful case"[13]—but either way Paneloux refused to call a doctor. If death was the will of God, a priest of God could not go against that will.

Camus's indictment was bitter, for of course to worship a god who was presumed to be the author of the plague was to worship evil. The Jesuit, whose hobby was the ancient pagan inscriptions around Algiers, was engaged in demonology not theology. Later, in a short story published in 1957 in *Exile and the Kingdom*, "The Renegade," Camus portrayed another priest, one who was captured by savages and who by slow and inevitable stages shifted his allegiance from his brand of worship of the supposedly Christian God to worship of a "fetish" of suffering and death. The horror and the mad logic of the absolutely parallel shift was vividly depicted.

In *The Plague* Camus arrived at what was to be his most distinct dichotomy in his portrait of natural forces.

On one side was the plague, a natural evil, with allies among mankind in such personalities as the murderous criminal and black marketeer Cottard. On the other side there gradually formed a little group of determined people, whose characteristics were not at first clear but became more distinct as Camus developed his theme.

Dr. Rieux and his friend Tarrou were the leaders. Tarrou was the ex-revolutionary who in youth had revolted against the government, in which his father was a prosecuting attorney. The establishment killed, and to be on the side of death was for Camus the ultimate allegiance to evil.[14] Then Tarrou discovered (as had the young Camus in his own revolutionary days) that the revolution also killed. Since that time Tarrou had decided to let the world have its wars and revolutions without him. Yet there was a curious quality to this state of detachment. It was probably endemic in the time of Camus. One may view it as a sort of psychological condition peculiar to the revolted and uncommitted in any violent ant heap.

In his fiction Camus was accustomed to using auxiliary characters who in no way advanced the plot but served as reflectors for other characters. For example, in *The Stranger* there was a little woman who moved like a machine, ate with mechanical motions, and marked a radio schedule with checks against the programs she intended to hear. She was a symbol of the automatized personality. "Rising, streetcar,"[15] and so on through each day's routine. In *The Stranger* also was an old man, Salamanno, who had a dog that he beat and dragged along the street, but who was desolate on the day the dog ran away. Salamanno was a man who had a negative relationship with the natural world but could not endure to be without it—a psychological condition that had deep affinities with that of Meursault.

In *The Plague* there were also two auxiliary characters. One was an old asthmatic patient of Dr. Rieux. The asthmatic spent his days putting peas one at a time from one pan into another. Like the woman who marked her radio programs, he was an automaton. The other auxiliary character was an old man who each day came out on his balcony, enticed a group of cats to come near him by dropping bits of paper, then spat on the animals and returned indoors. On the day the cats disappeared because of the plague, he was as desolate as Salamanno had been over the loss of his dog. The asthmatic was usually seen through the eyes of Dr. Rieux. Dr. Rieux had been accused early in the book by a young man in love of having the habit of dealing in abstractions.[16] The scientific doctor, who had been unable to think of how to say good-bye to his wife, was lacking in the more explicit forms of passion (one thinks of Sartre). His patients may indeed often have seemed to him like so many peas. When Camus introduced the man with the cats into his story, the narrator was usually Tarrou. The wanderer, Tarrou, who had inveterate curiosity and kept a notebook of odd facts (for example, the old man and the cats) maintained with the world a relationship of detached observation by his own bits of paper, his notes. Although Tarrou had as much contempt for humanity and for the universe as the old man had for the cats, he was attached to the very world he despised. Like the old man in *The Stranger*, Salamanno, he could not get along without it.

These ambivalences Camus saw as characteristic of a certain dynamic in modern development. He made a preliminary exploration in *The Stranger* of what he supposed the dynamic to be as he had seen it from 1938 to 1942. Meursault's passage from detachment and automatism on through lucidity and into scorn was what gave Camus his story. The story of *The Plague* was quite different. Tarrou had achieved lucidity and scorn before the book ever opened. Camus, who in 1942 had called Sisyphus "happy," was in 1947 quite obviously far from wanting his reader to apply that term to Tarrou in the condition in which the wanderer was introduced into the book. Unlike Meursault, Tarrou was in spite of his detachment a man of compassion and a seeker. The word he gave for what he sought was "comprehension."[17] Camus depicted him as ultimately finding what he sought through the plague.

The book opened with a portrayal of Oran's automatized people glued like so many atoms into collusive solidarity under their governing bureaucracy. The bureaucracy blinded the people to the truth; the people wished to be blinded. Camus depicted the twentieth century's automatism and its solidarity as naturally concomitant. When one increased, the other increased also. A certain kind of alienation and a certain kind of solidarity fed upon one another.

As Camus described the human condition in *The Plague*, the only solvent of alienation was love, the rare kind of love that caused a person to care more about the welfare of another than he cared about his own. Sartre in all his explorations of "being with others" had never examined any phenomenon that made a human being have deeper psychological concern for another than he had for himself. It seems doubtful that Sartre believed such a phenomenon existed. In any case he conspicuously did not write about it. In *The Plague* Camus wrote about little else.

There were eight main characters in *The Plague*—nine, counting the populace of Oran as a character, which Camus seemed to do in his numerous descriptions of the actions of the "people." Of the nine characters all but one, Cottard the black marketeer, underwent the same type of reversal. For example, Joseph Grand, a municipal clerk, who was a man of absolutely no significance in the eyes of his fellow townspeople and whom Camus's narrator, Dr. Rieux, called "the hero"[18] of this account of human anguish, was an alienated man whose preoccupation with his routine job in the bureaucratic ant heap had caused his young wife to leave him years before. Since then, Grand had been at work on a novel, a romantic novel, judging from the first sentence: "One fine morning in the month of May an elegant young horsewoman might have been seen riding a handsome sorrel mare along the flowery avenues of the Bois du Boulogne."[19] Grand kept changing this wording, never managing to get past the opening phrases, as he continually reworked the expressions with which one day he hoped to cause his imaginary publishers to say reverently, "Gentlemen, hats off!"[20] Man's search for perfection never found a more touching or more ironic image than in Camus's creation of this municipal clerk turned would-be novelist.

Grand formed part of the team which collected around Dr. Rieux to fight the plague. Grand's job was of course a clerical one. He kept track of the deaths. He remained matter-of-factly at his post until he himself was plague-stricken. For some time, as the plague had advanced, Grand had been thinking more and more frequently of his lost wife. Now, as the end of his life seemed at hand, he realized that his love for Jeanne had been his one vital experience. He then asked that his pile of manuscript be burned. Thus the "hero," Joseph Grand, passed into understanding of himself and the universe, an understanding previously concealed from him by life in the ant heap. More important than his job, more important than his doomed quest for perfection, was the simple human love he had lost.

Camus showed the same journey out of the numbness of the ant heap into the vitality of understanding the nature of love occurring over and over under the lash of the plague. Rieux's colleague, the aging Dr. Castel, had a marriage that had never gone smoothly. But when the plague broke out, Mrs. Castel, who had been away on a trip, returned to join him. In the "sudden glow" of their discovery that they could not live apart, "the risk of plague seemed insignificant."[21] Among the people of Oran men "who had pictured themselves as Don Juans became models of fidelity."[22] Even the bureaucratic magistrate, Othon, who had trained his children as if they were "poodles,"[23] underwent a similar reversal. In his relations with the townspeople, Othon's contention had been that officials never made mistakes. But Othon's little son Jacques was the child whose death Camus depicted. Afterwards, Othon, kept overtime in a quarantine camp, humbly admitted that officials did make mistakes and, in his new empathy for the plague-stricken, he joined Rieux's team and worked with

them until he died. Camus gave this transformed bureau-
crat the glory of martyrdom in truly loving service of the
plague-stricken people.

Oran was for Camus a symbolic microcosm. There, as
in Camus's cosmos from the beginning, the awareness that
every human being was condemned to death was the central fact. The concern for one another that Camus showed
the people of Oran learning during the plague represented
the concern Camus believed that all the world's people
should learn under the lash of death, which awaits humanity without exception. The moral view of Camus developed
significant additions to Dostoevsky's thesis that each was
responsible for all. With Camus each was indeed responsible for all. Only in recognition of that fact could anyone
begin to understand how to live, but all were shielded from
recognition of the truth by the numbness of existence in the
ant heap. When the threat of death was recognized, however, that numbness fell away—as Camus illustrated in the
lives of Grand, Castel, Othon, and the populace of Oran.

Death, which Camus had once seen as man's bitterest
enemy and the greatest injustice in an absurd world, he
now saw as serving the cause of vitality. Camus did not go
so far as to call evil in its guise as death good, but he did
arrive at the position that there were circumstances in which
death as threat could break open the death-in-life in which
most people existed in modern society. Death had a function in humanity's most essential spiritual growth. This
function was to cause mutual concern, which gave rise to
the genuine solidarity of a people open to one another, instead of the artificial solidarity of mutual blindness and

personal insularity which had held sway in bureaucrat-
ically governed Oran when the plague began.

Thus it was the plague that brought Father Paneloux
out of his detached and superior attitude toward the people
he supposedly served. In his first sermon he called them
remotely "you," while in his second sermon he addressed
them as his brothers and spoke of "we." It was the plague
that made the journalist Rambert decide not to escape to
join his sweetheart in Paris but to stay and work with
Rieux and Tarrou. He knew that if he went away he "would
feel ashamed of himself, and that would embarrass his relations with the woman he loved."[24] He understood that if
he abandoned the people of Oran he would so alter his
character as to change his relations with his beloved when
he rejoined her. Camus thus obviously disagreed with Sartre about the quality of individual life. According to
Camus, Rambert would carry his past with him and be
modified by it. Camus was quite correct in his frequent as-
sertions that he was not and had never been an existentialist. He was an absurdist who wrote himself out of belief
in absurdity and into belief in the existence of meaning in
the universe.

This meaning was for Camus a dualism of which the
universe itself, the whole state of being, was part. On the
one hand was death and evil, represented by the plague;
on the other, was love, brought into increasingly vital existence by each onslaught of death. For Camus good and
evil were thus opposites that acted upon each other in a
state of coexistent simultaneity. The universe that loosed
the plague upon humanity was at the same time, by the

very attack of the plague, also arousing the love which fought death, the love which was for Camus the supreme value. With Camus, as with Sartre, any person with a persistently linear consciousness may be unable to experience the full implications of his thought. For Camus, good did not merely in sequence and in reaction follow evil. Good and evil co-existed and good came into being through evil.

For example, Dr. Rieux continued to be a dutiful and slightly detached man of medicine and Tarrou continued to be an uncommitted observer in search of comprehension until both recognized the simultaneity of good and evil. This recognition developed gradually, but the moment of complete "comprehension" came when, after the death of little Jacques Othon, Tarrou made the suggestion, adopted by Rieux, that they should no longer only fight the plague by working to heal the sick but should also recognize that the plague was latently present in everyone in the city. Therefore, even the well were potentially sick in a universe where infection forever coexisted with health. It was then that Tarrou and Rieux determined to organize their "sani-tary squads," which by quarantine and other measures would protect the healthy against contamination.

Immediately after this decision Tarrou and Rieux went together for a night swim in the sea. Camus evoked the water he loved: "They saw the sea spread out before them, a gently heaving expanse of deep-piled velvet, supple and sleek as a creature of the wild."[25] The two immersed them-selves and swam together out from shore. The lyrical inten-sity of the passage expressed the unity both between the two friends and with the water that enclosed them. "Rieux lay on his back and stayed motionless, gazing up at the dome of sky lit by stars and moon. He drew a deep breath. Then he heard a sound of beaten water, louder and louder, amazingly clear in the hollow silence of the night. Tarrou was coming up with him . . . they swam back slowly, except at one point, where unexpectedly they found themselves caught in an ice-cold current. Their energy whipped up by this trap the sea had sprung on them, both struck out more vigorously."[26] To appreciate the passage one should turn to the end of the book: "The plague bacillus never dies or disappears for good . . . the day would come when for the bane and enlightenment of men, it would rouse up its rats again and send them forth to die in a happy city."[27] These were the words with which Camus ended his parable. They echoed of course the words of Caligula: "I am still alive."

For Camus nature was both evil and good. The two aspects were indissolubly linked and existed in inseparable simultaneity. However, the simultaneity of good and evil which Camus depicted carried no implication that the natural universe ever "cared" for man. The universe had only the strong suppleness of the sea, a "creature of the wild." As Camus saw it, the cold currents in the sea spurred man to swim faster. The psychologist Abraham Maslow learned from his patients that people were driven to highest fulfillment by striving against the most difficult obstacles. So Tarrou, Rieux, and all the people in Oran developed their beings against the horror of the plague. It was precisely the uncaring, destructive plague in Oran that gave birth to its opposite: the mutual concern and love that were for Camus the supreme value—as freedom was for Sartre.

Thus the duality of nature was reflected in humanity. In *Caligula*, the emperor personified the tyrant-rebel, who revolted against—and imitated—the evil of indifferent nature. Among the men and women of Oran were accomplices of plague. In Cottard, criminal and black marketeer, Camus no doubt saw the collaborator with the Nazi enemies of France. But to Camus the Nazis were only one type, though perhaps the supreme type, of the human carriers of the evil he symbolized by the plague. Opposed to the plague were what Tarrou called the "healers," the "saints without God." For Camus, the healers were generated by love, somewhat as for Sartre the autonomous person surged up out of freedom. Love and freedom were respectively avatars of the loving personality as seen by Camus and the free personality as seen by Sartre.

There is no doubt that both men had an orientation that must be called "religious." Each had a strong sense of the sacred. The autonomous person, as seen by Sartre, carried freedom within himself, just as the loving person, as seen by Camus, carried love. The fact that love was the supreme value for one and freedom the supreme value for the other did not disguise the fact that both regarded value as the creative source of the vitality of the race.

Just as both men had a sense of the sacred, both had a sense of the demonic. For Camus as for Sartre it was negation. One might call it "antivalue." For Sartre the inauthentic person was a person without sincere values. For Camus the unloving person was a Meursault, as Meursault appeared in the early stages of *The Stranger*, a creature with a semiparalyzed consciousness, in which values were

almost totally indistinguishable. For Sartre, the fact that
the universe was without value, that matter was opaque,
unreflexive, and absolutely unaware (an *"en-soi,"* an "in
itself" instead of, as for self-reflexive man who knows his
own existence, a *"pour-soi,"* a "for-itself"), gave the coexisting free and aware person a sense of nausea, horror—
the sort of emotion humanity had felt in other places and
at other times in regard to whatever it saw as forces of
mystery and darkness. There is an element of primitivism
in "nausea" as experienced by Sartre. The emotion seems
as undifferentiated, as untouched by civilization's clarity
and distinctness, as a bushman's instinctive dread of the
Kalahari night or a child's nameless horror in the dark. To
feel what Sartre meant by nausea one must peel back the
layers of habitual reassurance with which civilization has
insulated most of us. For Camus, too, nature in its indifference had a sort of horror. Father Paneloux spoke of the
plague as the scourge or flail of God. On hot summer nights
Dr. Rieux felt an awed but stoical disgust as he seemed actually to hear that flail over the stricken town. Similarly,
Meursault experienced the brilliant sun—at his mother's
funeral and when he killed the Arab—as having a sort of
malignance, while in "The Renegade," Camus's story of
the devil-worshiping priest, the blazing desert became de-
monism incarnate.

For Sartre the inauthentic person was socially the typical creature of the ant heap. For Camus the unloving person was the same. In the inauthentic person and the unloving
person, Camus and Sartre were describing the ant heap
personality under different aspects. For Camus evil in the

human community was ant heap society at its extreme, the totalitarianism of *la peste brune*, the Nazi regime that obliterated the individual in the mass. For Sartre it was the same. He saw totalitarianism as Nazism. Later, however, he also saw a dead, unfree bureaucratization in modern communism. Anyone who has witnessed in actuality or on film a Hitler-inspired mob, an audience of identically upturned faces and arms raised in fascist salute, probably knows that the filling of Red Square on May Day with identically marching throngs, crimson flags held at exactly the same angle, and heads turned to the reviewing stand where the leaders are stationed, is the same phenomenon. Massed humanity becomes one. The ant heap incarnates itself in a single creature: *la peste brune* is *la peste rouge*. In much of the earth this creature is coming into existence, marking its incarnation by the symbolic mass pageantry in which the individual is lost in the mass as the mystic is lost in his God. It is indeed the mysticism of the modern mass religions. Camus and Sartre portrayed the atomized personalities that were both created by the ant heap and sustained the ant heap, the fearful monster of their time with its own element of the demonic.

Yet Camus and Sartre did not despair. Camus predicated the simultaneous growth of interpersonal love over and against the plague, existing at the same time as the plague and stimulated by it. It was in knowing the disease of the plague, and more and more fully experiencing all that it meant, that Tarrou came to the "comprehension" he had sought for so long: the meaning of life was selfless service in the cause of life as "healer." Although Tarrou existed *within* the plague and it eventually killed him, what Camus implied by his symbolic parable was that wherever there was plague a Tarrou would also be shaped. What Sartre said was that the bureaucratized mass could not destroy the freedom of the young black who flew across the Channel. Both visions focused on the fact that in the simultaneity of opposites, one opposite (the massed ant heap) was inseparable from the other opposite (individuality growing against it and within it—for Sartre the sacred individuality of freedom, for Camus the sacred individuality of love).

Both men were fascinated by Dostoevsky, and one must see the Russian as their precursor. They differed from Dostoevsky, however, in that they placed their supreme value only in man and denied the existence of a transcendent godhead. But the unity in love and service that Camus depicted between Rieux and Tarrou during their symbolic swim had an undeniable transcendence. It was beyond the power of either man alone. It was also related to the natural universe which contained within itself that simultaneity of good and evil which, when they comprehended it, led Tarrou and Rieux to their most effective measures against the plague.

The difference between Camus and Dostoevsky in their views of good and evil is posited by the fact that in *The Plague* the swim of Tarrou and Rieux was initiated by them. Even though they did receive through it something of the same sense of mystical unity as was received by Dostoevsky's Markel and spread to others by Markel's moment of supernatural grace, Markel's grace was initiated by

God. That sort of initiative appears nowhere in the work of Camus.

However, when one considers the view of man's future held by Dostoevsky, Sartre, and Camus, one must note a startling resemblance. For Dostoevsky, Alyosha was the type of the future, a forerunner of humanity to come, as if the mystic and the saint were in fact mutations within the species, who forecast the future of the race. Teilhard de Chardin from the nineteen-twenties to the nineteen-fifties developed a similar hypothesis to much greater lengths. One remembers, however, what Dostoevsky said of Alyosha: that although "he carried within himself the very heart of the universal," nevertheless "the rest of the men of his epoch had for some reason been temporarily torn from it."[28]

Camus died in 1960. His last major book, *The Fall*, published in 1956, foresaw a sort of iron dictatorship of all against all, in which universally guilty men would forever convict all other men of guilt. Unable to achieve the unity of heart reached in *The Plague* by mutual concern, mankind was condemned by guilt to a unity that could come only through tyranny, "all together at last, but on our knees and heads bowed."[29] *The Plague* had been written in the surge of exaltation that nontotalitarians had felt at the defeat of fascism. For many that exaltation faded as communism turned out not only to have seized most of the fruits of victory, but also more and more clearly showed its own totalitarian character. It seemed to many that the chief result of the Second World War had been to turn over the Western part of Europe to the hegemony of the Soviet Union and to establish the dominance of Maoist China in Asia. For the author of *The Rebel*, that was a bitter perspective. Camus symbolized what he envisioned as the fate of humanity in his portrait of a world of "judge-penitents," creatures like *The Fall*'s antihero Clamence. A world of judge-penitents would be a world totalitarianism, with everyone on the same plateau, all judging those around them and being judged in return, a condition that was to be achieved quite notably in China during the era of the Red Guards.

The Fall drew for Camus an enormous and troubled audience. By the nineteen-sixties his works had been read by millions in every Western country, particularly by the young. He had equaled and for many had surpassed Sartre as the West's leading prophetic writer.

Dostoevsky died in 1881, thirty-six years before the Russian Revolution established a tyranny whose excesses were to cast those of the Tsars into the shade. Camus died in 1960, leaving as his final forecast of the future the vision of *The Fall* and its judge-penitents. In linear minds the fact that the pessimistic vision of *The Fall* came after the optimistic vision of *The Plague* was apt to mean that for Camus before his death pessimism canceled out the earlier optimism that had caused eight of his nine main characters in *The Plague* to undergo reversals which led toward Camus's supreme value, universal love.

To reason this way, however, is to forget Camus's vision of the simultaneity of good and evil and of the emergence of good from evil. There can be no doubt that Camus in 1956, the year of *The Fall*'s publication, saw humanity's

immediate future as dark. But the very fact that a visionary like Camus was moved by the gathering clouds of his
time to write such a warning as *The Fall* demonstrated the
formation of a good (the warning) out of an evil (the
darkening future) in that same simultaneity of good and
evil which in Camus's vision was characteristic of both
mankind and the natural universe. *The Fall* did not mean,
as so many believed, that Camus saw no hope for man and
was entering into a sort of Jansenism. A man without hope
could not have written that final vivid warning. One does
not warn those who one believes have no capacity to hear.
One shouts—and that was precisely what Camus, the former slum child of Algiers, the son of a deaf mother whom
he loved, was doing in the world of his time.

CHAPTER VIII

William Faulkner
and the
Tyranny of Linear Consciousness

Both Sartre and Camus were fascinated by the work of William Faulkner. The writer who in 1946, when Malcolm Cowley assembled *The Portable Faulkner*, had not a single major novel left in print and was earning his living as a scriptwriter in Hollywood, by the 1950s had a worldwide audience. In America six hundred thousand of his books had been sold in Random House and Modern Library editions, while the New American Library reported nearly five million in paperback—figures that did not include the tremendous sales abroad. Faulkner ranked with Dostoevsky, Sartre, and Camus as one of those who gathered and held enormous audiences.[1] In 1955 Camus adapted Faulkner's play *Requiem for a Nun* and it was produced in postwar France for an extended run and an enthusiastic

123

audience. Sartre's saying during the war years: "for the youth of France Faulkner is a god" had become more and more evident.[2]

Faulkner belonged to the tradition of James Joyce, who with Dostoevsky and Conrad was one of his favorite writers. The psychology of consciousness was an obsession for Faulkner. Obscurely, and yet with the stubborn certainty characteristic of his individualistic and nonconformist temperament, he felt that the linear thinking of the West was somehow inadequate, and in his writing he set out to explore that inadequacy.

America was, of course, the nation in which the linear causal mode of thought that gave rise to science and technology[3] had produced the greatest engineering feats on earth. In America the sheer majesty of technological achievement eclipsed intuitive vision of the relation between the humanity of the future and a gutted earth whose natural resources had been torn away in the blindest plundering that had ever taken place. All such primal and instinctive recognitions fell into darkness and silence before the predominance of "science" and "progress." A man like Faulkner, who in his novels dwelt on the sinister deforestation of his own Mississippi Delta, was viewed as odd, eccentric, atypical—as indeed he was, since the majority of his countrymen were furnishing the norm. As Jules Henry in his book on the United States, *Culture against Man*,[4] claims, the "drives" that urged Americans "blindly into getting bigger" were always victorious over the "values" of simplicity and instinctive quiet comprehension. In America skyscrapers went up to great heights simply to prove that such heights could be reached. Superhighways were often built less because of need than because of the riot of technology that invaded every area from transportation to human engineering.

Faulkner was born in 1897. He thus grew up in the period in which linear thinking was supreme in his nation's idea of its own character. Between 1776 and 1929 the original thirteen colonies had become a continent-spanning unity. Faulkner's youth was spent in a nation that believed devoutly in everlasting linear progress from less to greater.

And yet he was born in a section of that nation which could not wholehcartedly share that illusion. Faulkner's grandfather had fought in the War between the States. All around Faulkner's native town of Oxford were decaying Mississippi mansions which evoked a vanished past whose prosperity and magnificence were a dramatic contrast to the shabby present. As soon as Faulkner had a little money from his early books he bought such a mansion. Without plumbing, electric light, or heat, it was crumbling. Faulkner jacked up the massive building and by his own labor replaced the foundation. Whenever he had a little cash it went into more restoration at Rowan Oak.

The fact that many Southerners were like Faulkner in not sharing the American linear consciousness, the logical, rational, sequential, progress-oriented, and technological mode which in its crushing of perspectives born of intuition can become blind to past and future, may explain why so many of America's most clear-sighted writers came from the South. Faulkner certainly in his own mind did not impose linear succession upon human experience as if time were space and could be laid out along a measuring tape, but experienced time both as permeated by the past and as holding in embryo what is to be.

It took him many years to find out how to express the unusual aspect of his perceptions. At first he tended merely to create Southern antebellum stories like the early ones that made up the volume based on his own family's Civil War history, *Sartoris*. Then, quite suddenly in 1928, when the reception of his early novels had made him believe he would never achieve popular success, he began one day to write almost compulsively a description of what a totally nonlinear mode of consciousness which held past and present simultaneously might be like. With a burst of creative energy that was the keenest he would ever experience, he began to describe how the world appeared to Benjy Compson, a thirty-three-year-old man with the mind of a child. The disjunction between Benjy's experience of reality, the simultaneous reality of an idiot or an infant incapable of imposing succession upon time, and the contrasting linear experience of reality of those around him was an exaggerated portrayal of the difference between all linear consciousness and all states of consciousness not linear but simultaneous. Since most of us, however obscurely, share both states, one may look at the "grotesque," the idiot Benjy, and see in him, as in most grotesques in literature, the projection of an accentuated image of ourselves. Benjy makes us feel in magnified form a disjunction that many of us know. In Benjy past was completely undifferentiated from present. Any sensory signal could change his consciousness into any period of what for most of us would be memory—periods of love rejected, of longing unfulfilled, of happiness inexplicably removed. Benjy was the same age as Christ at his death. Benjy's life was a perpetual crucifixion, one we all share.

When Faulkner began the book he was thinking only of Benjy. But when he completed the pages portraying Benjy, he felt that it was necessary to go on and straighten out the time sequences of Benjy's experiences. He depicted in a second section the consciousness of Benjy's brother Quentin, a man under the tyranny of linear time and unable to endure it. Faulkner opened the Quentin section by describing how in Quentin's boyhood his father had given him a watch and said, "Quentin, I give you the mausoleum of all hope and desire . . . I give it to you not that you might remember time, but that you might forget it now and then for a moment and not spend all your breath trying to conquer it."[5]

Like Benjy, Quentin had known love only from one person, his sister Caddy, and like Benjy he lost everything that Caddy meant to him when inevitably in time she grew up, surrendered her virginity to a man she loved, married unhappily another man, and disappeared from the Compsons' view. No more than Benjy could Quentin endure the loss of Caddy, virgin and sister, embodiment of all that he valued. Quentin had ideals of honor, chivalry, purity, and love—the best remnants of the code of the antebellum Southern gentleman. In Faulkner's opinion these gentlemen had probably seldom or never actually existed, but their legendary exemplars, Jeb Stuart or Robert E. Lee, had left such an aching void where once glory, beauty, and heroism were supposed to have existed that, for those who shared the temperament of Faulkner's Quentin, the antebellum code was more present by its absence than it had ever been present in fact.

From the day of his father's gift of the watch, through which the former generation symbolically passed on its own sense of linearity, Quentin had learned more and more bleakly who the enemy of his kind was. It was irrevocable, implacable time. In vivid first-person stream of consciousness prose, as lush in its linear ongoing rush as growth and time themselves, Faulkner set forth the uselessness of Quentin's battle. At Harvard, after his sister's wedding to the man she did not love, Quentin ripped the hands off his watch. But, as his father had warned, the effort to stop time was useless. Throwing off the linear mode resulted for Quentin only in throwing off the logic on which depended coherent action in the present. Quentin fought with an acquaintance under the impression that he was fighting Dalton Ames, his sister's first lover. Finally Quentin cut short his anguish by the only recourse available to his species. He ended time by ending his own consciousness. He died by suicide, throwing himself into a river. Faulkner did not believe in personal immortality. Death was the great "obliteration."[6] By suicide Quentin would bring what he sought: the nothingness, the nonmotion he had hungered for all his short life. The mode of ending for the type of linear consciousness represented by Quentin was self-destruction, and death in a river—itself eternal ongoing motion.

In the next section of this book which Faulkner entitled "The Sound and the Fury," he turned from Quentin's type of linear consciousness to the type of linear consciousness he personally most abominated. This type of linear consciousness was shown in Benjy and Quentin's younger brother Jason to whom "time was money." The prose Faulkner gave Jason as narrator of his section was as characteristic of Jason's type of thinking as Quentin's prose had been characteristic of Quentin. Jason's words tumbled forth with the staccato barren bleakness of a despairingly matter-of-fact ledger written furiously in red ink. Jason rushed in frantic pursuit of a money-making future, which as constantly retreated just out of reach. He was a man in a frenzy of self-frustrating motion, always "too late" for the cotton market in which he speculated, always frustrated by circumstances. Promised a job by Caddy's rich husband, he was done out of that promise—"cheated," as Jason himself put it. Caddy's honesty and spontaneity would not let her stay with the man she despised.

Though Caddy saw most of her lovers through her longing to give and receive love and had opened herself to Dalton Ames because he could make her blood race, she was incapable of feigning. Of all the Compsons, only the passionate Caddy, beautiful and self-giving, lived in the present. She never entered the book as narrator but her personality pervaded it, right up to the moment of her last photograph, in which she appeared as the embodiment of the passion and doom that characterized humanity during this Compson generation. In Faulkner's later addition to his novel, the "Appendix" of 1943, "done," he said, "at the same heat as the book even though fifteen years later," he showed how he saw the later development of Caddy

Compson. He described Caddy's photograph, Caddy as last seen in 1940, as "beautiful, cold serene, and damned," the companion of "a handsome man of middleage in the ribbons and tabs of a German staff general." She "vanished in Paris with the German occupation . . . and was not heard of again."[7]

About 1911 Caddy had sent her illegitimate daughter, Quentin, home to grow up in what she hoped would be the security of her old family. But the money Caddy forwarded each month for young Quentin's support was embezzled by Jason. Frantically cashing and frantically hoarding each check as it arrived, he was outdistanced again by the everlasting flight of the fortune that eluded him. In 1928 young Quentin at seventeen, mistreated by Jason and hating her home, made off with the hoard and ran away in the night. After Benjy's suffering, Caddy's doom, Jason's frustration, and Quentin's suicide, Faulkner portrayed this Quentin of the next generation as presenting the contrast of utter lack of depth or consequence. Quentin ran off with a man from a circus carnival. His occupation was symbolic of this later era's triviality.

The final section of Faulkner's novel was told through the consciousness of Dilsey, the Compson family's Negro cook. The portrait was based on the Faulkner family's own Caroline Barr, to whom Faulkner in 1942 was to dedicate *Go Down Moses*, his book on the black community of his Yoknapatawpha County, his microcosm of the South. To Faulkner Caroline Barr represented so deeply and so essentially the values he cherished, that on her tombstone he caused to be engraved:

To Mammy
Caroline Barr
Mississippi
1840-1940
Who was born in slavery and who
gave to my family a fidelity without
stint or calculation of recompense
and to my childhood an immeasure-
able devotion and love.[8]

With the Dilsey section Faulkner's entire book became
an elucidation of the nonsignificance of linear time. Dilsey's kitchen clock was always three hours slow.[9] Chrono-
logically it always gave her the "wrong time," but time was
never "wrong" for Dilsey. She had an inner sense of the
passage of events that always told her what was actually
happening, and, far more importantly, her consciousness
held all time in simultaneity.

When one speaks to the average person about a consciousness in which all experience from first to last is held
in simultaneity, the reader or the listener is apt to believe
that such a consciousness must be like Benjy's, the consciousness of an idiot, or at least must do violence to particularity and individuality. But Faulkner was probably,
after Ibsen, the most determined advocate of individualism
that the West has produced during the last century. The
Benjy section, which Faulkner developed according to the
stream of consciousness technique he had learned from
Joyce, gave no physical descriptions. Nor did the Quentin
and Jason sections, in which he used first-person narration.
Faulkner reserved for the Dilsey section the startling emergence of these people in their physical reality. For the first

time Faulkner gave a physical description of Jason: ". . . cold and shrewd, with close thatched brown hair curled into two stubborn hooks, one on either side of his forehead like a bartender in caricature, and hazel eyes with black-ringed irises like marbles."[10] Even more startling was the emergence of Benjy: ". . . a big man who appeared to have been shaped of some substance whose particles would not or did not cohere to one another or to the frame which supported it. His skin was dead looking and hairless; dropsical too, he moved with a shambling gait like a trained bear. His hair was pale and fine. It had been brushed smoothly down upon his brow like that of children in daguerreotypes. His eyes were clear, of the pale sweet blue of cornflowers, his thick mouth hung open, drooling a little."[11]

The effect of these and other descriptions by the omniscient narrator, coming when the story was three-quarters over, was as if a bright light had suddenly been turned on, illuminating the Compsons as the reader had never seen them illuminated before. The Dilsey section was thus entirely different from the other three. The effect conveyed was that Dilsey lived in a world which possessed greater clarity, a special vitality, a deeper vision.

Dilsey's section opens on Easter Sunday, the Day of Resurrection. Dilsey takes Benjy to her Negro church. There a strange and compelling sermon by a visiting preacher begins, " 'Brethren and sisteren, I got the recollection and the blood of the Lamb!' " While a woman in the congregation exclaims, " 'Yes, Jesus!' " and Dilsey, with tears on her cheeks, sits with her hand on Benjy's knee, the preacher "like a worn small rock whelmed by the successive waves of his voice" speaks to the people who "did not mark just when his intonation, his pronunciation, became Negroid. They just sat swaying a little in their seats as the voice took them unto itself." He evokes the going out of Egypt. Then, with his accent becoming steadily more Negroid, his images more primitive, he speaks of the time of Christ, " 'Breddren! Look at dem little chillen sittin dar. Jesus was like dat once. He mammy suffered de glory en de pangs. Sometimes maybe she helt him at de nightfall whilst de angels singin' him to sleep; maybe she look out de do' en see de Roman po-lice passin.' " His voice rises; the people cry out that they too see Jesus. Dilsey sits by Benjy and weeps "rigidly and quietly in the annealment and the blood of the remembered Lamb." The preacher cries, " 'I sees it, breddren! I sees hit! Sees de blastin, blindin sight! I sees Calvary, wid de sacred trees, sees de thief en de murderer en de least of dese; I hears de boasting en de braggin: Ef you be Jesus, lif up yo tree en walk! I hears de wailin of women en de evenin lamentations; I hears de weepin en de cryin en de turnt-away face of God: dey done kilt Jesus; dey done kilt my Son!' "

Afterwards Dilsey, walking home with her family and Benjy, lets the tears roll down her face.

" 'Whyn't you quit dat, mammy?' her daughter asked. 'Wid all dese people lookin. We be passin white folks soon.'

" 'I've seen de first en de last,' Dilsey said. 'Never you mind me.'

" 'First en last whut?' Frony said."[12]

Frony, the average person, could not share the vision.

Dilsey's consciousness differed from all others in Faulkner's epic of types of human consciousness. She alone knew the simultaneous interconnectedness of all lives and all times. The bondage of God's people in Egypt, the presence of the Negroes sitting in their segregated church, the childhood of Christ, the crucifixion of the Son of God, and the innocent Benjy at Dilsey's side all coexisted so that she saw "the first and the last," all that has been and all that is, in the luminousness of eternity in which time, as most consciousnesses experience it, had no power to annihilate the relationship of all with all, of Dilsey's people with those bound in Egypt, of Benjy with Christ, and of every living being with every other. Dilsey's "I've seen the first and the last" was as incomprehensible to her daughter Frony as it is to most people. However to Faulkner, who created the epic, it may have been much the type of his own consciousness. A young Frenchman who interviewed him in 1953, and who was of course mindful of his nation's own enthusiasm for existentialism, reported that Faulkner, after saying to him that he disagreed with Sartre and Camus because it was wrong to do away with God, went on to express his personal idea of the basic nature of the ultimate reality. " 'I'm not talking about a personified or a mechanical God, but a God who is the most complete expression of mankind, a God who rests both in eternity and the now . . . a deity very close to Bergson's.' " He was reported to have added, " 'I agree pretty much with Bergson's theory of the fluidity of time. There is only the present moment, in which I include both the past and the future, and that is eternity.' "[13] It was a description that indeed owed something to Bergson, but the idea of a " 'present moment, in which I include both the past and the future, and that is eternity' " applied more accurately to the state of consciousness portrayed in Dilsey at the end of *The Sound and the Fury* than it did to the French philosopher.[14]

Faulkner emphasized the Negritude and the primitiveness evoked by Dilsey's preacher as he spoke. As the preacher left linear time and drew his congregation with him into simultaneous time, his voice lost the acquired resonances of the white people's world and fell into the archaic Negro patois. Apparently Faulkner saw simultaneous consciousness as belonging somehow to the primitive. In Jason, as in his brother Quentin, the evolution of linear thinking had eliminated the power to perceive reality as Dilsey perceived it. There can be no doubt that in 1928 in *The Sound and the Fury* Faulkner regarded Dilsey as a higher type of humanity than anyone else in the book. Nor is there any evidence that he ever changed his mind.

CHAPTER IX

Alienated Man
and the
Faculty of Categorization

America from 1840 to the present has been a land of cultural fragmentation. In a period in which all nations, all religions, all ethnic and cultural entities, all groups and particularities were clutching at bits and pieces of lost identities, the American fragmentation became prototypical of the world. In America more families moved every year than in any other country in peacetime. Cities, towns, and villages swarmed with "strangers." Furthermore, few Americans were more than three generations away from a foreign nation of origin. Faulkner's most conspicuous ancestor had crossed the Atlantic after the battle of Culloden in 1779, a background Faulkner gave the Compsons in his "Appendix." Long established though the Faulkners were in Mississippi, William Faulkner still felt that he was a displaced person. A friend said, "Faulkner saw himself as a Highlander living in exile in Mississippi. This attitude gave him, I think, an objectivity and a detachment about Mississippi, about the United States, which was one of the hallmarks of his conversation."[1]

Light in August, published in 1932, was a study of the attempts of alienated people to flee into some sort of solidarity, usually a pernicious, artificial, or evil solidarity. From the time Dostoevsky had analyzed the release each person felt who laid his freedom at the feet of the Grand Inquisitor, the typical counterpart of alienation had been believed to be the absorption of unbearable particularity into some kind of dictatorship. Faulkner's non-European mind knew nothing firsthand about dictatorship. He did know, however, multitudinous psychological routes by which his own countrymen got rid of freedom. He hated the earliest forms of "welfare state" that he saw beginning after the depression of 1929. Everything that sapped self-reliance, autonomy, or independence was to him an evil. But to Faulkner welfarism was merely the most overt solidarity of its type in the American diaspora. Far more damaging was the American faculty of erecting rigid and emotionally laden categories. The most conspicuous of these categories in Faulkner's period and place was the division between white people and black people.

The central figure in *Light in August* was Joe Christmas, an orphan with no knowledge of the circumstances of his birth. The white janitor at Joe's orphanage, who was actually Joe's grandfather, had implied to Joe before Joe was five that Joe was a "nigger," but Joe was parchment

colored and treated as white by the orphanage's administration. The goal of finding out whether he was white or
Negro became an obsession for Joe. Whether Joe was in
fact black or white Faulkner never revealed. Perhaps this
was intended to indicate to his reader the actual nonsignificance of the categorization that distorted Joe's doomed
life. In Joe Christmas, Faulkner created an exaggerated
reflection of the alienated and rootless man, for whom
category, in which the rootless person hoped to lose alienation and find solidarity, was a substitute for normal human relationships.

Joe was adopted by a Scotch Calvinist farmer,
MacEachern, for whom religion supplied a categorization
of all people into the damned and predetermined to sin,
and the elect and predetermined to everlasting bliss. Faulkner gave a description of MacEachern and Joe, as the
farmer took Joe to the stable for a beating because Joe
would not learn his catechism. "The boy followed, down
the hall, toward the rear; he too walked erect and in silence, his head up. There was a very kinship of stubborn-
ness like a transmitted resemblance in their backs . . . They
went on, in steady file, the two backs in their rigid abnega-
tion of all compromise more alike than actual blood could
have made them." After the beating Joe, who rejected the
catechism until MacEachern beat him unconscious, stood
"erect, his face and the pamphlet lifted, his attitude one of
exaltation. Save for surplice he might have been a Catholic
choirboy, with for nave the looming and shadowy crib, the
rough planked wall beyond which in the ammoniac and
dryscented obscurity beasts stirred now and then with snorts

and indolent thuds." Nothing could have been less like the earth-related simple naturalness of the animals than the rigid exalted Joe. Of this experience Joe always thought later: "*On this day I became a man.*"[2] MacEachern was a sort of priest of life-denying rigidity, who initiated Joe as his acolyte. Through MacEachern the need which Joe, as alienated being without home or roots, had for solidarity developed into a need for absolute rigidity. In his refusal of the catechism, Joe was the reverse of MacEachern but exactly like him. The development affected even his capacity for that most intimate and natural of all relationships, the sexual relationship between men and women. When some other boys had intercourse in a shed with a Negro girl and Joe took his turn, he beat the girl viciously. Not only did she violate his need for categorization of black and white, but by this time femaleness itself was a category for Joe, one he conceptualized in such a way that he could not accept it. As a child of five in the orphanage, Joe had hidden in a closet in order to feast on stolen toothpaste. He loved to lay the toothpaste in strips on his tongue. The toothpaste belonged to the orphanage dietitian (Faulkner's offbeat and perhaps sometimes unconscious humor in these situations recalls Joyce) who returned unexpectedly to her room with her lover, a young intern. While the two had hasty intercourse, the hidden child continued to put strips of toothpaste into his mouth until he vomited and was discovered.

For weeks Joe, who had no conscious awareness of the significance of what he had seen, waited to be punished for stealing the toothpaste. Punishment had the predictability his formless life relied on for security against chaos. He longed for the moment of retribution. However, his whole framework of predictability collapsed when the dietitian, instead of punishment, offered the child a dollar. Joe "was still with astonishment, shock, outrage," until the dietitian finally screamed, " 'Tell then! You little nigger bastard!' " The dietitian then "became quite calmly and completely mad. She no longer planned at all. Her subsequent actions followed a kind of divination, as if the days and unsleeping nights during which she had nursed behind that calm mask her fear and fury had turned her psychic along with her natural female infallibility for the spontaneous comprehension of evil."[3]

Faulkner was quite serious about the female's psychic comprehension of evil. For Faulkner, as for many men, the female was the obscure, the instinctive, the unpredictable side of the human race. Faulkner was happiest in male-female relationships when he could link himself with a much younger woman, preferably one who regarded him as teacher or sage or both, and so gave him a role in which he could exert an exaggerated dominance over his partner. This was his relationship with his young mistress Joan Williams, with the great friend of his older years, Jean Stein, and with his adored daughter Jill. With all three he found a happiness that eluded him with his individualistic and independent wife. But in Faulkner's fiction the unpredictable female with psychic powers did not always have an affinity for evil. She could have instead a psychic affinity for good, as Dilsey had. Dilsey was attuned to the sacred simultaneity that transcended categorization.

The dietitian, however, was no Dilsey. She used her psychic powers differently. She sensed there was some relation between Joe and the janitor. She drew from the old man mysterious references to "bitchery and abomination," which referred not only to herself but also to Joe's mysterious background tainted with supposed Negritude. By telling the matron that Joe was in the category: Negro, the dietitian got him put out for immediate adoption. That was how he came under the influence of his foster father, MacEachern, who supposed him white.

The distortion of Joe's capacity for any relationship with a woman was increased by Mrs. MacEachern. Her husband was cold, linear, predictable, rigid—as Joe himself came to be. MacEachern was entrenched in his alienated rigidity, which gave him dominance and security. For her own self-preservation, and from the need to cling to some remnant of free identity, Mrs. MacEachern had become as much a creature of deviousness as her husband was a creature of rigidity. As Faulkner saw it, the female's natural mode of coping with the rigidity of a MacEachern was deceit. Mrs. MacEachern brought Joe food when he had been sent to bed without dinner and tried to set up a hidden collusion between the boy and herself.

A further step in the distortion of Joe's capacity for any relationship of mutual trust with a woman came when at eighteen he fell in love with a prostitute named Bobbie Allen, a waitress in the nearby town. In the ballad, *Barbry Allen*, a man died of love. In a sense Joe also "died of love" in his meeting with Bobbie Allen. Bobbie's unforeseen and to Joe incomprehensible desertion confirmed Joe's

division of men and women into forever separated and
rigidly enclosing moral categories. Males were predictable. Females were lethally devious. A relationship between them was a relationship between opposites who must
be enemies. Faulkner's diagnosis of the war between men
and women was one more aspect of the destructive lust
for categorization he portrayed as characteristic of alienated persons.

For fifteen years after his experience with Bobbie
Allen, Joe tried to fit himself into some form of comforting
categorization. He "lived as man and wife with a woman
who resembled an ebony carving."[4] He lived as a white man,
as "laborer, miner, prospector, gambling tout; he enlisted
in the army, served four months and deserted and was never
caught."[5] At thirty-three (Faulkner liked to show his sufferers as being the same age as Christ at his crucifixion),
Joe came to the town of Jefferson, where he discovered the
woman who was his natural partner. Appropriately named
Joanna, this woman, by her family heritage, had also been
infected by the rigid categorization of black and white. She
was the descendant of white emigrants from the North, who
were obsessed by a creed of white guilt. They felt that
whites owed a duty to blacks in return for centuries of injustice and exploitation. There was nothing humane in
Joanna's concern for the blacks. No person-to-person compassion had a share in her performance of duty. She sat at
her desk dealing in pieces of paper for scholarships for
black students and donations to black organizations. Her
Calvinistic father, who had inherited the code of the early
abolitionists in distorted form, had taught her that every

white child was born as if on a black cross, bearing the
burden of guilt for the plight of the exploited blacks, a
"race doomed and cursed to be forever and ever a part of
the white race's doom and curse for its sins."[6] After that
Joanna, whose last name was Burden, seemed to herself to
see Negroes "not as people but as a thing, a shadow in
which I lived, we lived, all white people, all other people."[7]
It was categorization at its most extreme, a conceptualization that was absolutely rigid and lifeless. It absorbed Joanna's freedom. Her work in the cause of black liberation
was not chosen but compulsive.

Joanna was as hard and as rigid as any man when Joe
started to live in the cabin on her land. When Joe forcibly
possessed her it was "as if he struggled physically with another man for an object of no value to either, and for
which they struggled on principle alone."[8] The peculiar,
rigid, and utterly nonpersonal fusion between Joe and Joanna continued through complex and perverted convolu-
tions until Joanna, having experienced menopause and
repenting her sins, became determined that Joe should take
up her burden with her. As a Negro, he was to go to a Negro college and train himself to be her lawyer. But Joe,
whose rigidity had resisted MacEachern's, was not about
to fall to Joanna's. The crisis came when she evoked his
ancient traumas by asking him to pray with her. "It's because she started praying over me," he said that night in
his cabin. He went out and compulsively roamed the white
section of town; then as compulsively he went to the black
section, and reexperienced his inability to belong to either.
Finally he stood outside Joanna's house. Faulkner did not

show Joe thinking, deciding. For both Joe and Joanna, rigidity and categorization had utterly destroyed freedom. Joe's action now, the most important of his life, was completely predetermined. It had been determined before his birth by the impossibility of his fitting into either one of the two most rigid categories of his time and place, white or Negro. His thought before going into Joanna's was not "I can . . . or I will . . ." It was only, "*Something is going to happen. Something is going to happen to me.*"[9] With these italicized words Faulkner, who knew how to deal in suspense, broke off this portion of his narrative.

Faulkner had not begun *Light in August* with Joe and Joanna. He began with their opposite, Lena Grove. The name "Lena" was the diminutive of Helena, for the Greeks a word expressing beauty, luminousness, "the shining one." Grove evoked for Faulkner probably the pagan idea of the sacred. The Greeks had their temples in groves. Often a holy place was simply "the grove." In any case, Faulkner surrounded the figure of Lena Grove with a sense of the sacred. He made her a combination of Christian madonna and pagan earth goddess. Joe Christmas's initials, J.C., and his age, thirty-three, obviously implied that Joe was a figure of man crucified. But in Faulkner's cosmos in *Light in August*, salvation in no way rested with the crucified. It rested with Lena, the earth goddess of simple, natural, and easy human interrelatedness, who was immune to categorization of any kind. Lena was a country girl traveling in search of the man by whom she was pregnant and in whose desertion she refused to believe. Lena was quite a bit like Dostoevsky's Alyosha Karamazov, of whom one of Dosto-

evsky's characters had said that he could be put down anywhere on earth "without a penny," and "he would be fed
and sheltered at once. . . . And to shelter him would be no
burden, but, on the contrary, would probably be looked on
as a pleasure."[10]

Everyone sheltered Lena. Farmers gave her lifts in
their wagons and a hard-bitten farm wife even broke open
the china rooster in which she kept her egg money (another nice bit of comic symbolism). But most conspicuous
among Lena's helpers was Byron Bunch, the bearer of another of Faulkner's humorously meaningful names. Byron
suggested romantic illusions and Bunch, ordinariness. He
was one of any "bunch" of human beings. The union between Lena Grove and Byron Bunch, the earth goddess and
the average man, was Faulkner's creative counterweight to
the union of mutual destruction between Joe and Joanna.

Lena was shown as the redeemer of those whose existence she touched. Byron was a man perilously near a flight
from life. His mode of escape was work. He labored all
day at a planing mill and on weekends went to a country
church to rehearse its choir, returning only in time to get
back to the mill on Monday. Also bent on escape from living, escape in a more extreme mode, was Byron's friend
Gail Hightower. Hightower was a minister who had come
to Jefferson years before, not because he wanted to serve a
parish but because Jefferson had been the scene of his
grandfather's Civil War "charge on a chickencoop," a
phrase in which Faulkner expressed his contempt for this
sort of idealization, though it was an idealization he himself shared. The "charge on a chickencoop" of Faulkner's

ironic image stemmed from the real and entirely serious raids made by Confederate troops on Grant's stores.

Hightower's insistence on living in his dream of the past had driven his wife to promiscuity and finally to suicide. It had lost him the respect of his parish, to which he preached about galloping dragoons instead of about God, or rather about the two in inextricable confusion. It had lost him any part in life in the present. This was the sort of portrayal which made Faulkner so appealing to French existentialists, and often prevented them from knowing that he was not their precursor or fellow discoverer but had his own vision which belonged to another culture and a different orientation. On the day Hightower was turned out of his church, he came down the path holding an open hymnbook to cover his face; "Behind the book his lips were drawn back as though he were smiling. But his teeth were tight together and his face looked like the face of Satan in the old prints. The next day he brought his wife home and buried her."[11] If this man's detachment had driven his wife to destroy herself in such a way that he was now completely isolated morally from the community of feeling, suffering human beings; if he was now also being driven from his vocation and his livelihood into utter solitude; and if he nevertheless smiled, it was because isolation and solitude were perversely what he most desired, that he might have no other existence than in his illusions of the past.

It was a syndrome quite different from any diagnosed by Sartre. Life-denial was for Faulkner the mode of the alienated person's flight into an artificial and pernicious solidarity with illusion, the demonic opposite of that natural and sacred solidarity with the actual he had shown in Dilsey. Byron Bunch was an alienated man who found his illusionary sense of solidarity in work. Gail Hightower was an alienated man who found his artificial solidarity in imagining himself in union with a past that never was. Symbolically Lena drew both men back into life. Byron Bunch fell in love with her and left his job to look after her. Hightower, who had refused for thirty years to take any part voluntarily in the life of the town, delivered her baby, whom Joe Christmas's half-demented grandmother saw as her "little Joey" born again, to have another and better try at life.

On the same night that Lena Grove arrived in the town where she was to give birth, Joe Christmas was heading toward his final doom. Entering Joanna's house, Joe found Joanna sitting in bed with a gun concealed under her shawl. She fired but the ancient gun did not go off. Meanwhile Joe lunged with a razor and slashed her throat so deeply that when she was found later and carried out of the house, her head turned around as if she were looking backward—as Joanna had all her life looked backward at the ancestors who had shaped her "burden."

Throughout *Light in August* Faulkner kept evoking by implication (the name of Joe Christmas, the psychic capacity for evil of the dietitian, the idyllic characterization of Lena) forces that existed within human life but were more than human both in their nature and in their power. As the mob gathered that was to hunt down and lynch Joe Christmas, this evocation of the supernatural became more explicit. During his flight, Joe openly appeared in a nearby town and although he was recognized no one stopped him. Joe thought, "Like there is a rule to catch me by."[12]

There was indeed a rule, as Faulkner saw the nature of things in the world of his time. The rule centered around the power of categories like "nigger" and concepts like "lynch." As the mob of human creatures, itself one united creature, called into being by the power of the ritual words "nigger" and "lynch," gathered and began to hunt Joe down, there suddenly appeared, as if called forth by the mob's formation, a young man named Percy Grimm. Grimm had always regretted that he was born too late to serve in the First World War. He had always wanted to represent an ideal and wear a uniform. Patriotism and order were his conceptual obsessions. At first he wanted to stop the mob from illegally breaking into the jail and lynching Joe. But when Joe broke away from the sheriff, Grimm became the leader of the hunt. "What he was was a Hitler Storm Trooper," Faulkner said, "but then I'd never heard of one then . . . I think you find him everywhere, in all countries, in all people."[13] As Grimm pursued Joe, Faulkner's descriptions began to portray directly the intervention of supernatural evil. Grimm unaccountably knew where Christmas was. Grimm moved "with that lean, swift, blind obedience to whatever Player moved him on the Board." "He seemed indefatigable, not flesh and blood, as if the Player who moved him for pawn likewise found him breath." Even inanimate objects were in the hands of the Player, whose puppet was Grimm. The car bearing reinforcements for Grimm "was just where it should have been, just where the Player had desired it to be."[14] Hightower, who was making his supreme involvement in actuality by sacrificing completely the detachment in which he had lived, cried out that Joe Christmas was with him in a homosexual rendezvous on the night of Joanna's murder. Percy Grimm's reply was in a voice "clear and outraged like that of a young priest . . . But the Player was not done yet." In Hightower's kitchen, Grimm shot Joe Christmas and afterward mutilated him with a butcher knife.[15] The ritual of horror that had begun in the orphanage had proceeded to its end. Categorization, rigid conceptualization are for Faulkner forces that summon up the demonic, a malign distillation flowing not only out of human nature, but out of the very earth. In calling this force "the Player," Faulkner indicates his view of the nature of evil. It is that which destroys human liberty and turns people into puppets. It is the bloodstained idol to which men run to lay down their freedom. The continuity of this view in the current of meditation on the human condition which we have been tracing ever since the time of Dostoevsky is obvious.

In the days after the death of Joe Christmas, Hightower, sitting in his empty house in the "lambent suspension of August into which night is about to fully come," has a vision in which he sees the past of his own ancestors, which has haunted him all his life and has been part of his present for years, and actual faces he has known, all as if on a great wheel. Strangely one "face alone is not clear." It blends with another. They fuse. Here Faulkner broke up Hightower's insight with dots to indicate its spasmodic and only partial clarity. " 'Why it's . . .' he thinks. 'I have seen it, recently . . . Why, it's that . . . boy. The one who . . .

into the kitchen where . . . killed, who fired the . . .' " Two faces had blended. They were the faces of Joe Christmas and Percy Grimm. Joe Christmas, who lived in rigid conceptual categories and became victim, was one with Percy Grimm, who lived in rigid conceptual categories and became executioner.

As the book began with Lena Grove, so it ended with her. The story was told by a passing countryman who gave her a ride. She was traveling on in pursuit of the still fleeing father of her illegitimate child. With her was the adoring Byron Bunch hoping, as he had hoped since he first saw her, to make her his own. Lena was uncertain, however. She liked traveling and had come a "right good piece,"[16] all the way from Alabama. She was now in Tennessee. Byron followed and we gather that if necessary he would follow forever.

As genre the book puzzles and annoys some readers. The tragedy of Joe Christmas seems deliberately undercut by the comic romantic ending. There is an effect of disjunction that many find unsatisfying.

This disjunction, however, was part of Faulkner's vision. Lena's indecision at the book's end marked the nature of her being, which was to be completely free and determine her own course. In Faulkner's world in *Light in August* there was a range of freedom. There were people who were absolutely predetermined by the categorizing and conceptualizing forces that shaped them: Joe Christmas, Joanna Burden, Percy Grimm, MacEachern, and those like them. There were people who were refugees from life but won through to greater freedom—as Byron rid himself of his work ethic and Hightower at least partially broke out of his obsession with the past (though there were indications in his "light in August" passage that he might return). The ultimate peak on Faulkner's scale of human freedom was Lena Grove, earth goddess, madonna, and mother of mankind's future.

Joe Christmas, Joanna, Percy Grimm, and those like them represented the linear, categorizing, conceptualizing side of human nature that was the source of evil. Lena Grove was Faulkner's contrapuntal contrast. She conceptualized not at all but lived wholly on the instinctive, psychic level. With Lena this instinctive, psychic female side was in no way like the dietitian's or Mrs. MacEachern's. Lena was the essence of all in nature and in humanity that was luminous and good.

When one compares Joe Christmas, Joanna, Percy Grimm, and MacEachern to Lena one sees a contrast reminiscent of the contrast in *The Brothers Karamazov* between Alyosha and Dostoevsky's other characters. Lena was less fully and realistically drawn than the rest. If Lena was somehow the bringer of a redemptive future for the human race, as her mother-madonna role with the new Joey seemed to indicate, she had an allegorical blurring of outline which seemed to show that her type was not yet defined but an emerging shape still being formed. The opening description of her as she arrived in the town conveyed the impression of a creature coming gradually into being, still in process of creation by the earth's "avatars" exemplified in the primitive mule-drawn country wagons that carried her. She "advanced in identical and anonymous and deliberate wagons as though through a succession of creakwheeled and limpeared avatars like something moving forever and without progress across an urn."[17] This comparison to one of Faulkner's favorite poems, Keats's "Ode on a Grecian Urn," had the effect of creating a fusion of opposites: motion and stasis. Lena herself was such a fusion, always in flight and yet at the same time in the perpetual stillness of her tranquil mother and earth goddess role. There is a resemblance to Dilsey's vision in *The Sound and the Fury* of the sacred unity of "first and last." There Faulkner gave the fusion of opposites to a mystical state of mind, while in *Light in August* he tried to give them to a personality. The result was that Lena existed as much as an archetype of a world in redemptive future fulfillment as the simple country girl she was outwardly supposed to be.

As one looks back on *Light in August* in the full retrospect of Faulkner's work, it is not easier but more difficult to appraise where Faulkner stood in his view of the future of humanity. Did he see the future as belonging to Jason, to the men of money and spoilers of the earth whom he would show in the Snopes tribe as it proliferated and took over from the families of the Old South who like Quentin Compson had ideals of honor and decency however unreal? Did he see the future as belonging to Percy Grimm, the "Nazi" he portrayed before Nazis preempted the front pages of the newspapers of his world? Was the mob and its puppet-master, the Player, the shape of the future? In a story written during the Second World War a character asked what would be left of America after Hitler got

through with it. "Or Yokohama or Pelley or Smith or
Jones or whatever he will call himself in this country."[18]
The phenomenon of categorization that Faulkner examined has changed in its outward forms since he wrote,
but not in its essential character. Most of us do not antic-
ipate a frankly Nazi regime in the United States or a victory of some communist or other totalitarian party. Our
drift toward totalitarianism is generally assumed to be more
subtle. The type of religious categorization Faulkner portrayed in MacEachern has diminished if not disappeared
during the dissolution of most of America's religiously
rigid groups, while the categorization of black and white
that obsessed Joe Christmas has undergone changes. However it would seem that in America, since Faulkner wrote
Light in August in 1931, categorization has been increasing rather than diminishing. In the nineteen-seventies one
hears not of mothers with needy children but of "welfare
mothers," and "welfare mothers" with placards identify-
ing themselves as such march in the streets. One hears not
of retired people but of "senior citizens," who are a rigid
class entitled to certain benefits in medical care and public
transportation but are not free to earn more than a certain
amount and are in fact excluded from any significant role
in most of the nation's productive life. Nevertheless, the
"welfare mothers," the "senior citizens," the "student,"
the "underprivileged child" (entitled to free lunches, extra tutoring, and the general contempt of nearly everyone),
the "black worker" (entitled to special promotion, extra
salary, and the usual dose of contempt that goes with privileges for the categorized), the "woman executive" (also

dowered with matching privilege and contempt), all are
growing in number and spreading as increasingly deper-
sonalized layers in the American ant heap, which as categorization has increased has become composed of less and
less people and more and more ants. The most sinister aspect of the categories is that people not only willingly but
eagerly exchange personal autonomy and responsibility
for the privilege of being looked after. Like the subjects of
the Grand Inquisitor and of Faulkner's demonic Player,
they find freedom and responsibility intolerable. Faulkner
hated every form of American collective from the WPA
on. He had seen in two world conflicts the effects of categorization when it was used as a weapon of war. Faulkner
saw America develop the most mechanized armies on earth,
in which the obliteration of personality was carried to
heights of frenzied anonymity never before equaled. In a
story written toward the end of the nineteen-forties, he portrayed a character remembering World War I: ". . . a four
year tunnel of blood and excrement and fear in which a
whole generation of the world's young men lived like frantic ants, each one alone against the instant when he too
must enter the faceless anonymity behind the blood and the
filth. . . ."[19]

It is here that one must see again the startling resemblance between the visions of the human condition as experienced by Dostoevsky, Sartre, Camus, and Faulkner. Each
man maintained in tension a similar pair of diametric opposites. Dostoevsky opposed the prophecy of Zossima to the
prophecy of Ivan. Sartre developed his paradox of existential freedom inserted within deterministic dialectical mate-

rialism. Camus described the saints without God and the totalitarian world of the judge-penitents. And Faulkner, a man whose vision of the future saw an America of Percy Grimm, Joe Christmas, Flem Snopes, and Jason Compson, also saw a land of Dilsey and Lena Grove. All four put freedom and natural human interrelatedness in opposition to nonfreedom and rigidity.

Faulkner's sense of the demonic, which he developed in his oblique portrayal of the Player in *Light in August*, and which appeared later even more openly,[20] was contrasted to the sense of the sacred with which he surrounded Dilsey and Lena Grove. But the quality of the transcendent in his writing was less man-centered than the types of transcendence characteristic of Sartre and Camus. Faulkner as a religious writer was closer to Dostoevsky, although in spite of his occasional attendance at church and the use of Christian imagery in his writing, his thought did not in any literal sense fit religious orthodoxy. Like Sartre and Camus he used traditional theology as a matrix for new views and arrived at a fresh turning in religious thought, one not conformable to any past tradition but nevertheless a vision, dynamically a development of the religious consciousness evolved by past generations.

In his view of good and evil, Faulkner appeared less to resemble Dostoevsky, to whose mind the prophecy of Ivan and the prophecy of Zossima seemed to present themselves as an either-or, than he resembled Sartre and Camus, whose respective types of consciousness tended to bypass logical-linear contradiction and hold opposites in simultaneity, a mode Faulkner described in his work. He evokes the all-embracing consciousness of a Dilsey or the instinctive lack of linear logic of a Lena as existing at the same time and almost as a response to categorization and rigidity. As the forces of evil rise, so do the forces of good. While Joe Christmas is being hunted to his death, Lena gives birth to her child, the new humanity. The positive element in Faulkner's vision had at least as powerful a hold on his immense audience as the negative. The phrase for which Faulkner is most often remembered is his assertion in his Nobel Prize speech in 1950, that "man will not merely endure, he will prevail."

CHAPTER X

Simultaneity
and
Contemporary Cultural History

Since Wittgenstein, all claims for the accuracy of language have become so suspect that the suspicion must extend to literature. We all speak our "own" languages, and except in the case of mathematics the words we use seldom hold quite the same significance for two days or even two minutes in succession. Are not "stories" similarly suspect? Are they not like language also merely "games," which have no common characteristic but are "a complicated network of similarities overlapping and crisscrossing: sometimes overall similarities, sometimes similarities of detail"? Do we not have to say that there are in the world only stories, which are like language in having just vague " 'family resemblances,' " nothing really in common?[1] There is the story of Buddhism, the story of Christianity, the story of

157

American democracy, the story of Russian communism, the story of Chinese liberation of the Asian masses. In this view, world thought becomes a jumble of "stories," all equally true and equally false, with no means of even comparing one to another. Each culture, each nation, even each personality has its own "story."

But any claim that story actually shares so drastically in the fragmentation of meaning typical of our time is also suspect. There have been proven ways of relating story to experience. The mythic truth of story has been established by Jungian analysts with their patients. And surely we can now see that literature furnishes examples of the prophetic or self-fulfilling story. Anything that in our era enables meaning to widen its scope against fragmentation should be viewed as hope for development of a new coherence in understanding the history of human culture. As Viktor Frankl has said, what keeps each person alive and striving is discernment of meaning. Discernment of meaning is precisely what has been made most difficult by the fragmentation of thought during the present period of dissolving forms and crumbling systems.

It is in the context of establishing meaning over and against fragmentation that the correspondence between story and events that have actually come to pass may be valuable. As evidence here has shown, there have been stories which can be proved to have fulfilled themselves. Dostoevsky's "The Legend of the Grand Inquisitor" fulfilled itself in Germany, Russia, China, and indeed to some degree in most of the countries of the world. Sartre's story of freedom as an inescapable human condition fulfilled itself, especially and most interestingly in the vitality of freedom as an insurmountable insertion within bureaucratic marxism, a fact illustrated by the collapse of communism as a world monolith and in the dissent within the Soviet empire. Camus also created stories that corresponded with what has come to pass. Since he wrote *The Fall* in 1957, the vision of a totalitarianism supported by mutual guilt and repentance has fulfilled itself in the psychological orientation of Maoists, particularly since the time of the Red Guards. China's use of this sadomasochistic technique exceeds anything Arthur Koestler imagined in 1941 in his novel *Darkness at Noon*, based on Stalin's purge trials of the Old Bolsheviks. Meanwhile Faulkner's story of the perniciousness of which linear consciousness is capable, compared to the beneficence toward which intuitive consciousness is striving, has also been fulfilling itself. Since the Second World War, Buddhist, Hindu, and other nonlinear modes of thought have been entering the West. On the scientific front, psychologists as separated as Robert Ornstein in the United States and A. R. Luria in the Soviet Union, have been discovering facts about the human mind which show the importance of hitherto unsuspected relationships between the faculties of the brain that measure space and time and the faculties that govern logical-linear speech. It is clear that we are only beginning to understand the workings of the mind.

The quality of human thought, and also the quality of human history, seem to be changing. To hold logically contradictory opposites in the mind, such as the belief that man has become more and more free at the same time as he has become more and more totalitarianized into an apersonal ant heap, is bound to seem to many people simply abnormal. To imagine such a union of opposites in simultaneity can seem mad. But Jean-Paul Sartre's thought held precisely such a simultaneity, and he was not mad. Both Camus and Faulkner experienced opposites in simultaneity, and they were not mad.[2]

It may help to borrow from Robert Ornstein an elementary exercise that uncovers some of the characteristics of human consciousness. Ornstein in his book *The Psychology of Consciousness* asked his readers to think of their bodies as having right and left sides, to close their eyes, and to ask themselves the following questions, pausing after each to reflect carefully and "sense inside for the answer."

1 Which side of you is more feminine?
2 Which is more masculine?
3 Which do you consider the "dark" side of yourself?
4 Which side is "lighter"?
5 Which is more active?
6 Which is more passive?
7 Which side is more logical?
8 Which is more "intuitive"?
9 Which side of you is the more mysterious?
10 Which side of you is the more artistic?

"If you are right-handed," Ornstein wrote, "most likely you felt the right side of your body as more masculine, lighter, active, and logical, the left side as more feminine, dark, passive, intuitive, mysterious, and artistic."[3] This difference is due to the fact that in right-handed people the left hemisphere of the brain dominates. In left-handed people the right hemisphere dominates. With both males and females in our culture, there is a general ascendancy of the masculine, lighter, active, and logical over the feminine, dark, passive, intuitive, mysterious, and artistic. No reason can be discerned as to why the two hemispheres of the human brain took on these separate characteristics, or why one side dominates rather than the other in most people. These findings have simply proved themselves to be typical of the majority. It may be that in our society logical-linear thinking has crushed the intuitive more in men than in women, but in our male-dominated world the survival of the intuitive even in women has often been precarious. There has been in all cultures in the West a downgrading of the dark and intuitive side controlled by the recessive hemisphere and an upgrading of the light and logical side controlled by the dominant hemisphere.[4] The Latin word for left, "sinister," passed into language as having connotations both evil and mysterious. The French word for left, "gauche," has meant awkward. And, similarly, during all recorded history women were regarded as inferior beings, whose perceptions in practical logical-linear situations could be discarded or ignored.

Yet, paradoxically, from earliest times there was also respect for the psychic powers of the female half of the race. In ancient Greece the oracle of Delphi proceeded from the Pythia, the visionary who inhaled the sacred fumes which came from the earth in the temple of Apollo. In the Old Testament Deborah was a prophetess. Faulkner's Dilsey and Lena Grove were both female, both intuitive, both antilogical, and both psychically in touch with hidden and transcendent truths invisible to those around them.

The psychologist Carl Jung, who held that all mankind was united through the collective unconscious, which all shared and to which all contributed, also held that every male had a female side or "anima" which he ignored at his peril. The proper incorporation into the male personality of its anima—dark, intuitive, hidden, and usually unconscious—was for Jung of supreme importance for healthy individuation. According to Jung, "permanent loss of the anima means a diminution of vitality, of flexibility, of human kindness."[5] It is interesting that Jung, whose long career of original contributions to Western thought extended from his break with Freud in 1911 to his death in 1961, should have said loss of vitality, even of creativity might result from suppression of a man's anima, and particularly that he also mentioned "human kindness." In Jung's description, the anima seems to have much in common with the openness to change, the vitality, and especially the tenderness of mutual concern that Dostoevsky, Camus, and Faulkner believed necessary to human relationships. Each saw a natural human solidarity based on concern as opposed to an artificial solidarity based either on political tyranny or on categorization of human beings into sections within the ant heap.

The anima, as the female side, links itself naturally to the type of consciousness associated with the left side of the body and the suppressed right hemisphere of the brain. The Chinese, who like many peoples of the East, never until recently had the logical-linear mode that resulted in technology and the most severe type of linear orientation, had for many centuries a design that to them symbolized the male and female forces, the yin-yang. Below is the Chinese symbol of the yin-yang opposites.

There are three ways of looking at this design. One is to see its left and dark side as behind the right and light side. Another is to see its right and light side as behind the dark side. Either of these views is a superimposition, in which one of the opposites prevails over the other. At first glance, however, as the eye traveled ahead down the page, and before the linear and logical mode of habitually analytic consciousness was suggested, the design may have been seen on this page simply as one whole. Furthermore, even after the design separated into two halves, a usually logical-linear observer merely by staring at the design may be able to bring simultaneity back into awareness, and then the ease or non-ease with which the design can be maintained as a whole as opposed to the persistence of the tendency to impose one opposite over the other may be a measure of the capacity consciously to hold opposites in simultaneity. Thus, although most people today are conditioned to evoking logical-linear analysis, in which opposites usually collide and one is subordinated to the other, the yin-yang design may serve as an illustration of the fact that simultaneity does still for many people naturally occur—at first glance, so to speak—even though within a few seconds the logical-linear mode of habitual analysis may take over. But then the logical-linear mode itself can be suspended, to enable recovery of the initial, more simple, holistic way of seeing.

This sort of suspension of the logical-linear mode occurs with many of Sartre's paradoxes. Unease is often felt at first over the idea that man is "condemned to be free." But with Sartre, even the most logical-linear mind usually becomes in time habituated to paradox, and the peculiar Sartrean unity begins to seem natural. In the end even the most drastic of his paradoxes, the insertion of existential freedom within the determinism of dialectical materialism, may be accepted. Similarly, Camus's vision of the saints without God and his vision of the judge-penitents may at first collide. In Camus's work one aspect may seem to retreat behind the other as in the Chinese design. The idea of the judge-penitents may eclipse the idea of the saints without God, or the idea of the saints without God may seem to eclipse the idea of a world totalitarianism of judge-penitents. There is a frame of mind, however, in which both can be seen as integral to Camus's thought—as indeed they were. In *The Plague* it is the rise of the disease symbolizing evil and totalitarianism that calls into being the saints without God and their alliance consecrated in the primal waters of the sea. Similarly with Faulkner, the Dilsey and Lena Grove motifs may be seen as dominant and may be regarded as the background for Faulkner's statement in his Nobel speech that "man will not only endure, he will prevail." Or the Joe Christmas and Percy Grimm motifs

may be seen as dominant and contradictory to the affirmation of the 1950 speech. Actually, Faulkner held both motifs, and each strengthened the other, as is obvious from
the balance between the Joe Christmas story and the Lena
Grove story in *Light in August.*

Faulkner, Camus, and Sartre, therefore, each had the
type of consciousness able to hold opposites in simultaneity. All three saw the future of humanity as becoming increasingly totalitarian and unfree, but at the same time
becoming more free and developing spontaneous modes of
human interrelatedness. It is easier to say in words what
this contradiction does not mean than what it means. It
does not mean that if the totalitarian bureaucracies, which
in one form or another at present control most of the earth,
spread and finally enclose the entire globe, there will be
growing within this totalitarianism a bud of freedom and
natural unity, and that some day the totalitarian shell will
crack open to reveal the bud within. This is simply a linear
mode of thinking. It fits the vision of Dostoevsky but never
could accord with the visions of Sartre, Camus, or Faulkner.

According to these latter, both the human solidarity of
relatedness and freedom, and the political solidarity of
alienation and nonfreedom, are growing *at the same time.*
There are facts in the cultural history of our era that tend
to support these perceptions. For example, few in the West
would deny that China is a rigidly bureaucratized state
with emphasis on political unity and ant heap conformity.
Yet there is a supposedly "historical" and "dialectical"
work of art current in China today which shows clearly the
emphasis that the Chinese are simultaneously placing on

mutual concern as a purely human value. In the famous
Ballet of the White-Haired Girl, so popular that even school
children perform scenes from it,[6] the solidarity expressed
is supposedly a solidarity entirely of political praxis—the
people have overthrown the landlords. But at the same
time the dancers express a mutual concern for one another
that at the very least has to be termed humanistic and at
most can be regarded as a form of mystical unity, not only
between the people but also with the landscapes of mountains and sky that are shown as forming their background.
Winter snow is the setting for the doomed and cruel social
system in which the landlord kills the virtuous old peasant.
Hostile nature in the mountains, to which the white-haired
girl flees, reflects the brutality of the landlord's household
where she has been beaten. In the two last acts trees in leaf
and peasants with baskets of fruit greet the girl's lover and
his comrades as they return after the successful revolution.
It is possible simply to see the pathetic fallacy as being
used for stage effect, but the feeling seems to verge toward unconscious natural mysticism, in which nature, as
with Camus, is seen as carrying the forces of both good
and evil in union with the human beings it encloses. At the
end, the rise of a crimson sun in a glorious sky reflects the
red banners of the victorious young soldiers in an effect of
unity with the cosmos. This appears to be expressed entirely without the awareness that it is an old and basically
theological convention. Throughout the ballet, history appears as the vessel on which man embarks to work out his
fate. To the authors and choreographers, the rising crimson sun of a new day for humanity after the revolution was

no doubt good marxism. It was also one of the most
ancient forms of man's sense of sacred unity between humanity and the universe. Meanwhile tenderness from person to person, for example the sympathy of the older maid
in the landlord's house for the white-haired girl, was like a
rebirth of a feeling expressed centuries before, "See how
these Christians love one another." The Chinese are officially an atheistic people, but their art expresses both a
feeling of cosmic unity and a feeling of human interrelatedness in which mankind has for thousands of years felt a
sense of the holy.

Visitors to China report evidence of love and service
among the people. Their devotion to the welfare of all as a
sacred cause seems most movingly genuine. Although the
Chinese tourist bureau no doubt is as careful to preselect
what may be seen as Russia's notorious Intourist, and although refugees bring accounts of Chinese prisons for political dissidents that are as hideous as similar reports from
Russia, these facts only make more keen the contrast between opposites in Chinese life. Within a system run by a
bureaucracy and backed by terror there is selfless giving.
A recent visitor reported conversations beneath whose obvious propaganda can be sensed a depth of dedication that
reflects emotions most people have traditionally reserved
for the holy. The effect is a dissonance in which both notes
are genuine. There is the repellent one-sidedness that exists
in all propaganda and the attractive openness of a loving and giving personality. This dissonance has been experienced by every visitor to Russia, but to see it repeated so
exactly in Russia's enemy is significant. Carol Travis, who

went to China in 1974, reported: "The director of the Women's Association of the Chin-An district in Shanghai sees her husband two weeks a year, since he works in another city. They send each other study materials on Mao Tse-tung Thought because 'our common purpose is to build socialism and consolidate the proletarian dictatorship.' I asked her how she feels about the separation. (Patient smile.) 'We do not regard separation too seriously as a bad thing. We accept it as necessary for the good of the country . . .' The rhetoric sounded familiar, and I probed for the woman underneath. 'I was a child laborer before Liberation,' she said. 'I mean it.' "[8]

Similar impressions of the coexistence of opposites are conspicuous in Russia. That the regime is totalitarian is a fact that for decades has been for most people in the free world beyond dispute. That within Russia there has been simultaneously evolving a sense of human community that has grown with as well as against the regime is the opposite phenomenon, one that our linear minds often suppress. The Russian movies *The Cranes Are Flying* and *Ballad of a Soldier* contained scenes as beautiful and probably as unnoted in Russia for their evocation of natural mysticism as similar scenes in the *Ballet of the White-Haired Girl* were unnoted for the same aspect in China. In the two Russian films, love, as the deepest element in human solidarity in situations of trial and separation, was as conspicuous as in any portion of Camus's *The Plague*. In a slightly different way the Russian Yuri German's prewar novel *The Cause You Serve* showed a Russian doctor on the desolate fringes of civilization giving service as selfless as that undertaken by Camus's saints without God.[9] A recent traveler to Russia, however, saw great changes in the people he had met on a previous trip in 1970. An older woman, the head of the Moscow Intourist Bureau seemed to him to have genuine devotion to communism. She seemed sincere in claiming that she would accept any assignment that would be a channel for her desire for service. Her childhood memories were of her life under Tsarism. But many young people, on the contrary, seemed self-serving, eager for the relatively easy life of Moscow, and very much afraid of being sent into outlying areas, not at all like the self-sacrificing Russian doctor Yuri German wrote about three decades earlier. This traveler's impression was that self-giving and devotion in Russia had by 1970 largely passed into Russian resistance to the regime.[10]

Certainly it is true that in the Russian resistance there appears to be a genuine sense of concern and of commitment to one another even at the possible sacrifice of life. This was shown, for instance, by the support the rebel physicist Sakharov publicly gave his fellow rebel Solzhenitsyn. There seems to be growing in the Soviet Union's underground a person-to-person solidarity of care and mutual protection that is the antithesis of what might be expected of human relations in a police state. Solzhenitsyn himself in his *Letter to the Soviet Leaders* has shown not only an opposition to the tyranny and apersonalism he attributes to technology, but an almost Tolstoyan belief in the unity of the good between people who are simply and naturally open to one another. Indeed, so dedicated is he to the practice of this belief that it is the spirit in which he addresses the Soviet leaders.[11] The unity Solzhenitsyn felt for his land and its people was tellingly demonstrated by the vigor with which he fought exile. He was ready to give up life itself rather than his homeland, although nothing could be more detestable to him than the Russian tyranny. Here appears again the typical dissonance between opposites growing against each other. Person-to-person openness grows against its opposite, apersonal state dictatorship. Meanwhile fervent patriotism and genuine love of country grow against a government that is crushing the country. Each of the opposites is intensified by the friction between them.

Is there in America any such friction between opposites? Does the United States have any simultaneity resembling that in the Soviet Union and China? For Americans to open their intuitive faculties to their own possible simultaneity of opposites and expect to cancel out linear thought about what is closest to them is no doubt particularly difficult. Yet cannot anyone in the United States see that, as mobilization for the Vietnam War fed forces of bureaucratization until many citizens came to think of themselves as computerized numbers, in that same period of the 1960s openness from person to person became almost an obsession, particularly among the young? In regard to the development of consciousness of mystical unity, it is scarcely possible in any American city today to throw a stone at random and not hit a roshi or a rishi or a guru who is teaching ways of experiencing no-mind, satori, or any of the multitude of techniques which try to reach the unity of all with all. These practices were imported from the nonlinear thinking of the East and are in complete contradiction to the linear and technological traditions of Americans of past generations.

There are other more everyday indications that linear thinking may have reached and passed the peak of its exclusive preponderance. We may be entering an era in which even the everyday actuality in which we live can be effectively influenced only by a consciousness capable of understanding and experiencing simultaneity. Only persons aware of simultaneity may be able to act effectively within the reality into which the world is now emerging. The very condition of chaos, in which the linear, tradition-oriented particularities of race or culture are breaking up, causing alienation and the desire for solidarity which feed mutually on each other and produce new categorizations and rigid separations—this condition of Western culture. to which most still free personalities cannot adjust, is forcing the emergence of a new kind of personality that *can* adjust. The linear security of religions, nationalities, professions, ethnic societies, and other tradition-minded and progress-oriented groups has been uncomfortably diminished. But these types of categorization developed at a time in history when they were necessary for the survival of the race. Huddling into traditional religious, national, and ethnic identities has served to protect individuals during the individualistic period dating approximately from the Renaissance, when the chief problem of mankind was the ongoing warfare of all against all. Similarly, logical-linear thinking developed the scientific technology that was necessary for the survival of mankind against hostile nature. Today's problem is not so much how to subdue nature as how to heal and make peace with it. In personal relations the problem is no longer how one individual or group may keep another individual or group from outright attack, but how to interrelate all in the peaceful coexistence of opposites by interconnectedness, tolerance, and the exclusion of collision over world problems that is characteristic of that frame of mind we have called simultaneity.

In its primitive state human consciousness was more intuitive and nonlinear than it became in technological societies. That was why Lena Grove and Dilsey were "primitives." Perhaps in such figures there may be seen an evolutionary spiral in which primitive nonlinearity may be regarded as having been in hidden passage through and behind the linear stage before coming out on a higher level, to foreshadow the intuitive and spontaneously interrelated humanity that may surpass and leave behind our present fragmented condition.

Dostoevsky, Sartre, Camus, and Faulkner brought insights from the instinctive and intuitive side of human nature into a clarity open to the intellect. Dostoevsky's Father Zossima explained a vision of human solidarity which was based on a mystical perception, one that was quite alien to logical-linear thinking. Dostoevsky made Father Zossima say that mankind was like a sea and the effects of human action on one part of its waters vibrated to the farthest parts of the globe, and that his hidden sea would be victorious over obstacles of whatever kind. Similarly, Sartre's concept of an existential freedom which was enclosed, indeed hidden, inside determinism was alien to logical-linear thinking. His description of the effects of the action of the young black who stole the plane on others who heard of his action was much like Dostoevsky's description of the vibrations from person to person in the invisible human sea. Camus caused the searching wanderer Tarrou to discover his long-sought "comprehension" in a brotherhood that was actually celebrated by immersion in a symbolic and mystical "sea." Tarrou and Rieux, in their swim together, experienced their invisible unity with the cosmos and with all humanity in their fight against the plague. Faulkner's Dilsey, as she sat in church listening to the sermon that made her feel that she saw all time, "the first and the last," in unity, was also a figure experiencing a human solidarity that was usually on the hidden, suppressed side of consciousness. All four writers brought into daylight aspects of the hidden side of human existence.

Dostoevsky, Sartre, Camus, and Faulkner practiced art in such a way as to make it in effect prophetic vision. Broad and substantial agreement exists among the four visions. There is also unity between those visions, and what historically took place soon afterward: the abrogation of freedom set forth in Dostoevsky's "The Legend of the Grand Inquisitor," which was fulfilled in totalitarianism; the psychology of mutual accusation which Camus explored in *The Fall*, which also came to be a favorite instrument of Maoism; the breaking up of the effectiveness of bureaucracy in the Soviet Union which Sartre foresaw in *The Critique of Dialectical Reason*, and earlier, in his play, *Dirty Hands*; and finally the sinister use of categorization as a dehumanizing force that Faulkner understood as an American obsession. Dostoevsky, Sartre, Camus, and Faulkner also believed that humanity, on the one hand, was moving toward a totalitarian political unity of the most oppressive kind but, on the other hand, was at the same time advancing into a freedom and openness never before achieved. These four visions were not only astonishingly alike but also seem to have fulfilled themselves in "truth," in the sense that truth is correspondence of the mind with an actuality, that is, with events that later came to pass. The work of Dostoevsky, Sartre, Camus, and Faulkner, therefore, goes beyond excellence of technique, beyond the ability to develop plot, character, or structure, into an excellence that consists also in having brought into open awareness a hidden flow of historical, cultural, and theological change. To ignore this aspect of art is to reveal lack of comprehension of some of the greatest visions of our time: why they arose, how they developed, and why they remain valuable.

The value of these visions centers on the diminution of linear thinking and the rise of simultaneity through the hidden side of both history and the mind. In simultaneity violence is greatly mitigated. In the ant heap in which, for example, love as envisioned by Camus or freedom as envisioned by Sartre exist inside an enclosing mass, there is no violent victory of one over the other. What ensues is a mutual penetration, an interconnection of opposites in an orchestration where one tune becomes absorbed by another, with the more vital melody eventually permeating and coloring the whole.

To recognize simultaneity is to recognize that good grows within negation, is stimulated by it, develops inside it and with it, as well as over and against it. To accept this fact takes courage because one must admit that the negation, which evil is, has arrived and is all-pervading, infecting every person and every nation.

Evil is a lack of being, a lack of good. To say that our time has developed apersonal societies reveals what in fact has happened. We have developed societies in which the personal element is missing or almost missing. The society is apersonal. It lacks personalization. Lack is negative. Love and freedom are positive. They are the vital melody within the dissonances of the massed neo-religions.

The world's future must shape itself increasingly as a great unity. Camus and Faulkner show love and freedom permeating that mass unity just as atmospheric oxygen or nitrogen from food diffuses in living tissue. For Sartre freedom surges up with a spontaneity that is a given of the human condition. Dostoevsky, in his Russian vision, would have seen love and freedom as divinizing forces. If Dostoevsky's terms are applied to modern simultaneity, love and freedom are indeed divinizing, while the massed societies, within which love and freedom grow by the perpetual stimulation of their opposites, are that which will be divinized. It is in fact the massed societies that provide the opportunity for fulfillment of that golden Byzantine dream of long ago, a sacred race living in unity on a sacred earth.

Humanity is unimaginably ancient. According to the discoveries at Olduvai Gorge, the skull of the prehominid Zinjanthropus is one and three-quarter million years old.[12] But only about three thousand years of human development can be traced by recorded history. Thus if hundreds of centuries still separate the human race from the golden vision, that separation is, on the great scale of things, a barely perceptible fraction in the advance of the human soul. Meanwhile what appears to sustain the contemporary mind best is a steady endurance in the face of enormous cruelty and desperate odds.

The essence of tragedy is the victory of man's spirit over man's fate. When Sophocles showed calamity attacking the world of Oedipus, there was born in the Western mind the vision of suffering man as he who endures and, though vanquished, is through his unconquerable vitality greater than his fate. Oedipus is blessed. He reappears at Colonus to affirm a new civilization. With the Christian tradition there comes into tragedy the Christian power to transmute suffering into greatness of spirit. In the religions of the East suffering is to be avoided by union with the infinite and indifference to the temporal. The West, however, sees suffering as the very road to union. The dying Lear is storm-battered, robbed of his dignity as a man, and torn from his one faithful daughter by her death. Yet as he comes out with the body of Cordelia in his arms, he is reborn into a fullness of love he could never have reached in his once secure life as king. Nor need recognition of the power of suffering to transmute human nature vanish in the massed societies of neopaganism. There is a tragic sense of life that combines the Greek and Christian modes. If we are mortal, says Unamuno, and if the Christian promise is at best a hope and at worst a lie, then let us so live as to indict that lie for its injustice. Let us live for the future of mankind on earth.[13] The glory of the tragic sense from its

inception in our race is its discernment of the power of the
human spirit to rise to a level at which it can thrust upward
with a strength created by the very adversities that drag it
down. Tragedy is an affirmation of the evolving universe,
for the spirit of man is the growing edge of life on earth.
The growth within man's own life depends on the evolution of his understanding. In every age there appear scattered insights that are advance ripples of future tides of
comprehension. Prophetic writers are the furthest forward
on the rising tide of humanity's self-knowledge. It is they
who unriddle the paradox that within the mass tyrannies
(which in man's inalienable liberty he is choosing in
our time) freedom and greatness of spirit are rising with
strength to match their bonds. There can be little doubt the
world is entering into a time of tragedy. What is to be
sought by minds today is not the pattern behind the calamity
of mass tyranny, a pattern that is only too well known, but
what should be examined and experienced deep within
every evolving consciousness is the counterthrust of the vic-
tories even now forming in our shadows.

N O T E S

CHAPTER I   Alienation and Solidarity,
Interlocking Opposites

1   The split began in the ninth century but solid links were reestablished
thereafter. The schism between Rome and Byzantium grew gradually
over a period of approximately two hundred and fifty years. For an extended account of the hostility against Rome as it grew in Russian religious thought and in Russian culture, see James H. Billington, *The Icon
and the Axe* (New York: Knopf, 1968). Dostoevsky's own account of
the character of the split is as follows: "The idea of the universal
Roman empire succumbed, and it was replaced by a new ideal, also universal, of a communion in Christ. This new ideal bifurcated into the
Eastern ideal of a purely spiritual communion of men, and the Western
European, Roman Catholic, papal ideal diametrically opposite to the
Eastern one. . . . We have in the Eastern ideal—first, the spiritual communion of mankind in Christ, and thereafter, in consequence of the
spiritual unity of all men in Christ and as an unchallenged deduction
therefrom—a just state and social communion. In the Roman interpretation we have a reverse situation: first it is necessary to achieve firm
state unity in the form of a universal empire, and only after that, perhaps, spiritual fellowship under the rule of the Pope as the potentate
of this world." Fyodor Dostoevsky, *The Diary of a Writer*, 1877 (New
York: Braziller, 1954), pp. 728-29.
2   Fyodor Dostoevsky, *Letters of Fyodor Mickailovich Dostoevsky to His
Family and Friends*, translated by Ethel Colburn Mayne (London:
Chatto & Windus, 1914), February 22, 1854, p. 59.

179

3 Alexandr Solzhenitsyn, *Letter to the Soviet Leaders* (Evanston, San Francisco, London: Harper & Row, 1974), pp. 23 f.

4 Fyodor Dostoevsky, *The Brothers Karamazov* (New York: Random House, Modern Library edition), p. 678.

5 Alyosha is twenty on page 14, nineteen on page 22. There must be a five-year interval between the births of Dmitri and Ivan to correspond to Fyodor's marriages, yet Ivan is twenty-four, while his elder brother Dmitri is twenty-seven. Dmitri was four when his father married Ivan's mother. See pages 9 and 14, Dostoevsky, *The Brothers Karamazov* (Modern Library edition).

CHAPTER II   Suffering and Psychic Blackmail, Dostoevsky and Sadomasochism

1 Ant hill or ant heap is Dostoevsky's term for the mass empire backed by a mythic and blasphemous religion that he believed would come to exist if what he called "socialism" triumphed in the world of the future. True to the Russian concept of Rome as the betrayer of the spirituality of religion, he saw the Pope as the leader of the ant hill: "On foot and barefooted, the Pope will go to all the beggars, and he will tell them that everything the socialists teach and strive for is contained in the Gospel; that so far the time had not been ripe for them to learn about this; but that now the time has come, and that he, the Pope, surrenders Christ to them and believes in the ant hill." Dostoevsky, *The Diary of a Writer*, 1877, p. 738. See also Dostoevsky, *The Brothers Karamazov* (Modern Library edition), p. 267.

2 Dostoevsky, *The Brothers Karamazov* (Modern Library edition), p. 116.

3 Ibid., p. 195.

4 Ibid., p. 121.

5 Ibid., p. 629.

6 Ibid., p. 701.

7 Dostoevsky had an affair with a proud woman who rather resembled Katerina Alexandrova, and she used to torment him by arousing his desire for her and then denying herself to him. Dostoevsky told her, "You cannot forgive me because you once gave yourself to me." The revenge motif he imputed to her was thus much like Katya's. Robert Payne, *Dostoevsky: A Human Portrait* (New York: Knopf, 1967), pp. 171-72.

8 The Stalinist terror, which caused the displacement of many of these people, was not a subject of the Western world's indignation or even of its awareness, a remarkable instance of mass blindness.

CHAPTER III   The Opposite Predictions,
Ivan and Zossima

1 Dostoevsky, *The Brothers Karamazov* (Modern Library edition), p. 140.
2 Ibid., p. 42.
3 Ibid., p. 129.
4 Ibid., p. 132.
5 Ibid.
6 Ibid., p. 137.
7 Ibid., p. 277.
8 Ibid., p. 288.
9 Ibid., p. 289.
10 Ibid., p. 69.
11 The name means "bearer of victory." Payne, *Dostoevsky*, p. 282.
12 Quoted by Edward Wasiolek in *Dostoevsky: The Major Fiction* (Cambridge, Mass.: M.I.T. Press, 1964), p. 163.
13 Dostoevsky, *The Brothers Karamazov* (Modern Library edition), p. 254.
14 Avrahm Yarmolinsky, *Dostoevsky, His Life and Art* (New Jersey: S. G. Phillips, 1957), pp. 356 f.
15 Dostoevsky, *The Brothers Karamazov* (Modern Library edition), p. 259.
16 Ibid., p. 262.
17 Ibid., p. 272.
18 Romano Guardini, "The Legend of the Grand Inquisitor," *Cross Currents* (Winter, 1954), p. 64.
19 Dostoevsky, *The Brothers Karamazov* (Modern Library edition), p. 246.
20 *Time Magazine*, March 18, 1974, p. 45.
21 Dostoevsky, *The Brothers Karamazov* (Modern Library edition), p. 300.
22 Ibid., p. 335.
23 Ibid., pp. 301, 317.
24 Ibid., p. 272.
25 Ibid., p. 380.
26 Quoted by Constance Garnett in the "Preface" to the Random House College Edition of *The Brothers Karamazov*, p. vi.
27 Dostoevsky planned a sequel to his novel and possibly Alyosha would have been more fully developed there. The whole work had long existed in embryo in Dostoevsky's notebooks as *The Life of a Great Sinner* and Alyosha was to be the central figure. After marriage and life in the world, he was to join the Nihilists and kill the Tsar. But at the end of his life he would retire to a monastery where he would become a saintly spiritual leader and teacher. As spiritual leader Alyosha was to carry on the mode of his "elder," Father Zossima. Payne, *Dostoevsky*, p. 372.

28 Dostoevsky, *The Brothers Karamazov* (Modern Library edition), p. 317.
29 Dostoevsky finished *The Brothers Karamazov* in early November, 1880,
    and died on January 26, 1881. See *Dostoevsky Portrayed by His Wife*,
    translated by S. S. Koteliansky (London: George Routledge and Sons,
    1926), pp. 232-33.

CHAPTER IV   Simultaneity of Opposites,
Jean-Paul Sartre

1   Jean-Paul Sartre, "Existentialism," translated by Bernard Frechtman, in
    Existentialism and Human Emotions (New York: Philosophical Library,
    1957), pp. 24-26.
2   Jean-Paul Sartre, *The Words*, translated by Bernard Frechtman (New
    York: Braziller, 1964), pp. 97-99. *The Words*, as an autobiography that
    ends at age eleven, caused some amusement when it was published.
    Actually the fact that the book gives such importance to the early years
    illustrates a thesis Sartre emphasizes. His biographies of Flaubert and
    Genet show the essential personality in its most decisive processes of
    formation during childhood. When the identity, "thief," was thrust upon
    Genet as a child, he defiantly assumed that identity—and kept it.
3   Ibid., p. 103.
4   Thomas Aquinas, *Summa Theologica*, I, 84, 5 (New York: Benziger,
    1947), p. 427.
5   Sartre, "Existentialism," pp. 14-15.
6   Jean-Paul Sartre, *The Flies* in *No Exit and Three Other Plays*, trans-
    lated by Stuart Gilbert (New York: Vintage, 1955), p. 56.
7   Ibid., pp. 60-61.
8   Ibid., p. 123.
9   Hermann Hesse, *Siddhartha*, translated by Hilda Rosner (New York:
    New Directions, 1951), p. 115.
10 Ibid., p. 122.
11 Sartre, *The Flies*, pp. 87, 89.
12 Ibid., p. 115.
13 Jean-Paul Sartre, *Being and Nothingness*, translated by Hazel Barnes
    (New York: Philosophical Library, 1956), p. 566.

CHAPTER V   Existentialism, Violence, and
Communism

1 Jean-Paul Sartre, *No Exit* in *No Exit and Three Other Plays*, p. 20.
2 Ibid., p. 44.
3 Ibid., p. 33.
4 This sort of bargain was reflected elsewhere in the drama of the period. Edward Albee in 1960 examined much the same situation when he dramatized the relationship between the American "Mommy" and the American "Daddy" in *The American Dream*. Daddy, who was impotent, was assured that he was virile by Mommy; while Mommy, who was sterile, was assured of her charms by Daddy's financial support and psychological subordination.
5 Sartre, *No Exit*, p. 46.
6 Ibid., p. 47.
7 Ibid., p. 45.
8 Jean-Paul Sartre, *Dirty Hands* in *No Exit and Three Other Plays*, pp. 224-25.
9 Ibid., p. 224.
10 Sartre in these years had a great dread of World War III.
11 Interestingly, 1951 also saw the final quarrel between Sartre and Camus in the publication of Camus's *The Rebel*, which like *The Devil and the Good Lord* viewed political rebellion as having metaphysical roots.
12 Jean-Paul Sartre, *The Devil and the Good Lord and Two Other Plays*, translated by Kitty Black (New York: Vintage, 1960), p. 149.
13 Alfred Fabre-Luce, "Un barbare parmi nous," *Aurore*, March 21, 1964.
14 Jean-Paul Sartre, *Critique de la raison dialectique* (Paris: Gallimard, 1960), p. 9.
15 The insertion of the "ideology," existentialism, into the "philosophy," marxism, follows somewhat the pattern in which Sartre in *Being and Nothingness* saw free man inserted as a splinter into the material world. There could be no doubt which was the more vital. In 1943 in *The Flies*, Sartre had Zeus say to Orestes: "You are a foreign body in the world like a splinter in the flesh . . ." p. 25.
16 Sartre, *Critique de la raison dialectique*, p. 25.
17 Ibid., pp. 65-66, 73.
18 That is to say, alienation in its active form as protest, not in its passive form as apathy.
19 "Tant qu'on n'aura pas étudié les structures d'avenir dans une société déterminé, on s'exposera à ne rien comprendre au social." Sartre, *Critique de la raison dialectique*, p. 66.

CHAPTER VI Albert Camus and the World of
the Absurd

1 Sartre, *The Words*, p. 88.
2 Albert Camus, *L'Envers et l'endroit* (Algiers: Charlot, 1937), p. 27.
3 Albert Camus, *The Plague*, translated by Stuart Gilbert (New York: Vintage, 1972), p. 229.
4 *The Stranger* had great vogue in France during the war but the height of its popularity in the rest of the Western world came during the postwar period from about 1946 to 1970, when a gradual waning in enthusiasm began to be noticeable, particularly among young people, many of whom were giving Hesse the place once occupied by Camus.
5 *The Stranger* grew out of an earlier unpublished work "A Happy Death," which Camus wrote in 1935 when he was only twenty-four.
6 Albert Camus, "The Absurd Man" in *The Myth of Sisyphus and Other Essays*, translated by Justin O'Brien (New York: Vintage, 1955), p. 50.
7 Albert Camus, "An Absurd Reasoning" in *The Myth of Sisyphus and Other Essays*, p. 10.
8 Albert Camus, "The Myth of Sisyphus" in *The Myth of Sisyphus and Other Essays*, p. 89.
9 Ibid., p. 91.
10 Albert Camus, *The Stranger*, translated by Stuart Gilbert (New York: Vintage, 1946), p. 76.
11 Ibid., p. 154.
12 When Caligula was leaving the palace to roam the countryside in his shock after Drusilla's death, a patrician asked what was amiss. Caligula replied in one word: "Nothing." Nothingness, no order of cosmic justice—only accident, mortality, and indifference—that was for Caligula, as for Camus, "what was amiss." In *Caligula* Camus explored the "wrong freedom" as answer to that condition. Metaphysical rebellion was already "wrong" for him and the wellspring of tyranny. Thus the quarrel between Camus and Sartre as soon as Sartre entered the frame of mind of *The Devil and the Good Lord* was inevitable. Albert Camus, *Caligula* in *Caligula and 3 Other Plays*, translated by Stuart Gilbert (New York: Vintage, 1958), p. 5.
13 Ibid., p. 62.
14 Ibid., p. vi.
15 Ibid., p. 73.
16 Ibid., p. 8.
17 Ibid., p. 7.
18 Ibid., pp. 8-9, 73.

CHAPTER VII   Absurd Reasoning
and the Saints without God

1 Camus, *The Stranger*, p. 18.
2 Ibid., p. 74.
3 Ibid., p. 63.
4 Camus, *Caligula*, p. 66.
5 Ibid., p. 36.
6 Camus, *The Plague*, p. 4.
7 Ibid., p. 48.
8 Albert Camus, *The Possessed*, translated by Justin O'Brien (New York: Vintage, 1960), p. vi.
9 Camus, *The Plague*, pp. 89-91.
10 Ibid., p. 192.
11 Ibid., p. 196.
12 Ibid., pp. 201-02.
13 Ibid., p. 211.
14 Later Camus and Arthur Koestler were to collaborate on an essay against capital punishment. For both Camus and Koestler the state as executioner of criminals was as guilty of murder as any individual who took up an axe in order to destroy life.
15 Camus, "An Absurd Reasoning," p. 10.
16 Camus, *The Plague*, pp. 79, 117.
17 Ibid., p. 120.
18 Ibid., p. 126.
19 Ibid., p. 96.
20 Ibid., p. 94.
21 Ibid., p. 64.
22 Ibid.
23 Ibid., pp. 26, 106.
24 Ibid., pp. 78, 188.
25 Ibid., p. 232.
26 Ibid., p. 233.
27 Ibid., p. 278.
28 Dostoevsky, *The Brothers Karamazov* (Random House College Edition), "Preface," p. vi.
29 Albert Camus, *The Fall*, translated by Justin O'Brien (New York: Knopf, 1957), p. 136.

CHAPTER VIII   William Faulkner and
the Tyranny of Linear Consciousness

1   Joseph Blotner, *Faulkner, a Biography* (New York: Random House, 1974), II, 1492.
2   Ibid., II, 1222. *Requiem for a Nun* was a disappointment when it was finally produced in 1959 in New York. It closed after forty-three performances. The London production, also with Ruth Gordon and Zachary Scott, had been a spectacular hit. Ibid., II, 1718.
3   I am drawing on Robert Ornstein's *The Psychology of Consciousness* (New York: Viking, 1972), to which the last chapter of the essay will refer at greater length.
4   Jules Henry, *Culture against Man* (New York: Random House, 1963), p. 14.
5   William Faulkner, *The Sound and the Fury* and *As I Lay Dying* (New York: Random House, Modern Library edition), p. 95.
6   Blotner, *Faulkner*, II, 1046.
7   Faulkner, *The Sound and the Fury*, p. 12.
8   Blotner, *Faulkner*, II, 1094.
9   Faulkner, *The Sound and the Fury*, p. 290.
10   Ibid., p. 295.
11   Ibid., p. 290.
12   Ibid., pp. 311-13.
13   Blotner, *Faulkner*, II, 1441.
14   As I understand Bergson's theory of the "durée," the past interpenetrates the present. "Pure duration is the form which the succession of our conscious states assumes when our ego lets itself *live*, when it refrains from separating its present state from its former states . . . in recalling these states, it does not set them alongside its actual states as one point alongside another, but forms both the past and the present states into an organic whole, as happens when we recall the notes of a tune, melting so to speak, into one another . . . We can thus conceive of succession without distinction, and think of it as a mutual penetration, each one of which represents the whole and cannot be distinguished or isolated from it except by abstract thought." Henri Bergson, *Time and Free Will*, translated by F. L. Pogson (New York: Harper, 1960), pp. 100-01. However, Dilsey's awareness during the sermon seems to be holding images from past and present in unison rather than experiencing a present which the past permeates. Dilsey was not present at the birth of Christ nor at the crucifixion, yet both exist for her, not

in memory, but as if she were witnessing them, while she is simultaneously witnessing the childlike innocence and the suffering in the life of Benjy, who is at her side.

CHAPTER IX   Alienated Man and the Faculty
of Categorization

1   Blotner, *Faulkner*, II, 1777.
2   William Faulkner, *Light in August* (New York: Random House, Modern Library edition), pp. 128-31.
3   Ibid., pp. 109-10.
4   Ibid., p. 197.
5   Ibid., p. 196.
6   Ibid., p. 221.
7   Ibid.
8   Ibid., p. 205.
9   Ibid., p. 103.
10   Dostoevsky, *The Brothers Karamazov* (Modern Library edition), p. 17.
11   Faulkner, *Light in August*, p. 59.
12   Ibid., p. 294.
13   *Faulkner in the University*, edited by Frederick L. Gwynn and Joseph L. Blotner (New York: Vintage, 1965), p. 41.
14   Faulkner, *Light in August*, p. 405.
15   Ibid., p. 407.
16   Ibid., p. 11.
17   Ibid., p. 6.
18   Blotner, *Faulkner*, II, 1065.
19   William Faulkner, *Knight's Gambit* (New York: Random House, 1949), p. 231.
20   William Faulkner, *The Wild Palms* (New York: Vintage, 1964), p. 264.

CHAPTER X   Simultaneity and Contemporary
Cultural History

1 Ludwig Wittgenstein, *Philosophical Investigations*, I, 66, translated by
   G. E. M. Anscombe (New York: Macmillan, 1953), p. 322.
2 It is perhaps necessary to stress the radical uniqueness of the simultaneity of opposites coming to pass in contemporary thought and contemporary culture. The resemblance to dialectic is superficial, as one
   must see if one scrutinizes closely the passages quoted from Sartre's *The
   Critique of Dialectical Reason*, which do not compromise with dialectic
   but constitute an attack on it. Indeed, to grasp how simultaneity oper-
   ates, it is necessary constantly to keep in mind that it is entirely different from any dialectic, whether of Marx, Hegel, or Barth. It is also
   distinct from what is called "process" in contemporary theological language. It arises, quite simply, whenever conceptual or historical opposites advance at the same time in an interdependent simultaneity.
3 Ornstein, *The Psychology of Consciousness*, pp. 50-51.
4 The division of the faculties associated with the two hemispheres, so far
   as our very limited knowledge of them at this time is concerned, is
   interesting. A. R. Luria has found that injury to the recessive right
   hemisphere has resulted in "severe loss of direct orientation in space
   and time," while the verbal processes in such patients (whose dominant
   left hemisphere is intact) developed into meaningless "verbosity, which
   bore the character of empty reasoning." Thus even the logical-linear
   processes lose coherence and direction, although they increase their
   activity, if the recessive hemisphere ceases its orientation in time and
   space. Meanwhile the logical-linear tries to "cover" for faulty or inadequate spatial and temporal orientation. The pattern seems to me much
   the same as that of many modern people whose intuitive faculties are
   oversuppressed or even impaired by long suppression, and who become
   extremely verbose and "logical" in their attitudes. See A. R. Luria, *The
   Working Brain* (New York: Basic Books, 1973), Section 167.
5 Carl Jung, "Concerning the Archetypes and the Anima Concept,"
   Collected Works (Princeton, N. J.: Princeton University Press, 1959),
   IX, 71.
6 Carol Travis, "Field Report: Women in China," *Psychology Today*
   (May, 1974), p. 45. Photograph of deaf-mute children performing the
   first act of *Ballet of the White-Haired Girl*, identified simply as "a revolutionary ballet." Many people in the United States are well acquainted
   with this ballet from having seen the 1972 cinematic version.

7   John K. Fairbank, "In Chinese Prisons," *New York Review of Books* (November 1, 1973), pp. 3-7.

8   Travis, "Field Report: Women in China," p. 45.

9   Yuri German, *The Cause You Serve*, translated by Olga Shartse (Moscow: Foreign Languages Publishing House, n.d.).

10 The traveler was Mr. Charles Greenleaf, a retired manufacturer from the Midwest. He spent three weeks in Russia, visiting Leningrad, Moscow, Kiev, and the Karelian Peninsula.

11 Solzhenitsyn, *Letter to the Soviet Leaders*, pp. 23 f.

12 *Visitors' Guide to Olduvai Gorge* (privately printed), p. 4.

13 Miguel de Unamuno, *Tragic Sense of Life*, translated by J. E. Crawford (New York: Dover, 1954), p. 268.

INDEX

191

About this book

   Dark Prophets of Hope was set in the composing room of Loyola University Press. The text is 12 on 14 Bodoni Book; the reduced matter, 10 on 12; and the notes, 8 on 10. The display type is Bodoni Book (Mono 875).

   It was printed by Photopress, Inc., on Publishers Matte 50-pound paper and bound by The Engdahl Company.